William Ralston Shedden Ralston

Early Russian History

Four Lectures Delivered at Oxford

William Ralston Shedden Ralston

Early Russian History
Four Lectures Delivered at Oxford

ISBN/EAN: 9783337168902

Printed in Europe, USA, Canada, Australia, Japan

Cover: Foto ©ninafisch / pixelio.de

More available books at **www.hansebooks.com**

EARLY RUSSIAN HISTORY.

Four Lectures

DELIVERED AT OXFORD, IN THE TAYLOR
INSTITUTION, ACCORDING TO THE TERMS OF
LORD ILCHESTER'S BEQUEST TO
THE UNIVERSITY.

By W. R. S. RALSTON, M.A.,

OF THE BRITISH MUSEUM,
CORRESPONDING MEMBER OF THE RUSSIAN IMPERIAL GEOGRAPHICAL SOCIETY.
AUTHOR OF "THE SONGS OF THE RUSSIAN PEOPLE," "RUSSIAN FOLK-TALES,"
"KRILOF AND HIS FABLES," ETC.

LONDON:
SAMPSON LOW, MARSTON, LOW & SEARLE,
CROWN BUILDINGS, 188, FLEET STREET.
1874.

CONTENTS.

CHAPTER I.
LEGENDARY RUSSIA 1

CHAPTER II.
SUBDIVIDED RUSSIA 39

CHAPTER III.
THE TARTAR INVASION 59

CHAPTER IV.
THE TARTAR YOKE 80

CHAPTER V.
TSARDOM 116

CHAPTER VI.
TROUBLOUS TIME 136

CHAPTER VII.
SUPPLEMENTARY 157

PREFACE.

DINNER in Russia is preceded by a *zakuska*, a snack designed to whet the appetite. The present volume is intended to act as a kind of literary *zakuska*. I trust that it may not be altogether unsuccessful in whetting the appetite of the reading public for Russian history: towards satisfying it so slight a book can, of course, render but scant service. There is little in the following pages beyond the text of four lectures delivered at Oxford during the spring of this year, and into four lectures no very exhaustive analysis of a large subject can well be compressed. They have been revised and re-arranged, and the last part has been re-written; but I soon found that if I once began to fill up the sadly manifest gaps in my narrative, I should probably never be able, with anything like satisfaction, to leave off. My principal aim has been to give a few pictures from early Russian history; to sketch the leading features of two or three of its most important periods, and so to produce certain general impressions upon the minds of readers who may not have the requisite time at their disposal for an exact study of its details. I have troubled them but little with my own opinions, but I have done my best to lay before them the judgments, on vexed questions, of the best and most recent among Russian historians. The histories of which I have made most use are those of Karamzin, Solovief, Kostomarof, and Bestujef-Riumin [1], but there are many other exceedingly valuable works, to which I would most

---

[1] Karamzin's history, especially in its French form, is so well known that I need not do more than allude to it. The references to Solovief in the present volume are to his *Istoriya Rossii* [History of Russia], Fourth Edition; Moscow, 1866, &c. More than twenty volumes have already appeared, but it is uncertain when it will be completed. Those to Kostomarof are to his most recent work entitled *Russkaya Istoriya v zhizneopisaniyakh*, &c. [Russian History in biographies of its most prominent characters], Parts 1—3; St.

gladly have referred if I had been able to have easy access to them.

The map which is inserted in the present volume was originally intended as a slight assistance to the hearers of my lectures. It does not pretend to anything like exactness, being merely a rough sketch-map designed to convey a few general ideas about Russian localities. I have added two lines of colour, in order to render intelligible at a glance the great change in Russia's area which took place during the Tartar domination. I may as well observe that in doing so, I profess merely to follow Russian maps, without giving any opinion as to points which may have given rise to political controversy.

Petersburg, 1873-4. Those to Bestujef-Riumin are to his "Russian History," of which vol. I. was published in 1872 at St. Petersburg. I may add to the list Pogodin's *Drevnaya Russkaya Istoria*, &c. [Ancient Russian History up to the Mongol yoke], 3 vols., Moscow, 1871, accompanied by an atlas containing some 200 engravings. Among smaller books to which I am indebted may be mentioned Petrushevsky's spirited " Tales about Old Russian Days " [*Razskazui*, &c.]. Fourth Edition; St. Petersburg, 1873.

RURIK AND HIS PRINCIPAL SUCCESSORS.

RURIK (862—879).
|
IGOR (912—945).
|
SVIATOSLAF (957—972).
|
VLADIMIR I. (980—1015).
|
YAROSLAF I. (1019—1054).
|
VSEVOLOD (1078—1093).
|
VLADIMIR II. MONOMACHUS (1113—1125).
|
GEORGE DOLGORUKY (1157—1159).
|
VSEVOLOD (1176—1212).
|
YAROSLAF VSEVOLODOVICH (1236—1246).
|
ALEXANDER NEFSKY (1252—1263).
|
DANIEL (d. 1303).
|
IVAN I. KALITÀ (1328—1341).
|
IVAN II. (1353—1359).
|
DIMITRY DONSKOI (1362—1389).
|
VASSILY I. (1389—1425).
|
VASSILY II. (1425—1462).
|
IVAN III. (1462—1505).
|
VASSILY III. (1505—1533).
|
IVAN IV. THE TERRIBLE (1533—1584).
|
FEODOR (1584—1598).

NOTE:—This list of ruling Princes is not complete. Continuity of descent has been preserved, but not (as the dates will show) of succession.

EARLY RUSSIAN HISTORY.

CHAPTER I.

LEGENDARY RUSSIA.

IN a book published not long ago a scholar, one to whose hands the moulding of many young minds is entrusted, has stated that the Slavonic races may do great things when they have "defecated their political existence of the Asiatic dregs of despotism and serfdom." But that in the meantime we cannot "even vouchsafe the name of history to the insignificant and bloodstained annals of their imperial autocrats."

But in spite of these hard words about the many millions of Slavonians with whom we may claim cousinship, I venture to hope that it may be possible to find some interest in the study of Russian history, to detect some traces of the picturesque, the romantic, and the dramatic elements in the scenes which it reveals, and to deduce some not quite unprofitable doctrine from the lesson which it reads as to the relations between moral causes and physical effects. There may be readers to whom these advantages do not appear to be sufficiently practical. But even they may consider it worth their while to obtain some aid towards understanding the present existence and foreseeing the future career of what is now one of the mightiest empires in the world, by studying its early history—by investigating its origin, analyzing its constitution, and testing the various influences under which it first came into being, then underwent a hard struggle for life, and afterwards, having shaken off its early enemies, commenced the series of successes which have extended its borders from the Baltic to the Pacific, from the frozen realms within the Arctic Circle to regions not far removed from our own Indian Empire.

I do not propose to attempt anything like a continuous tracing of this successful career, or a complete explanation of the historical problems which it involves. There are several explorers at work, some of whom are likely before long to bestow upon English readers the fruits of such an investigation of Russian history as can be carried out only under the most favourable circumstances as regards time and space. Mine is a far humbler undertaking: that of attempting to give prominence to a few of the most striking pictures which early Russian history presents, to explain some among the most important results which it chronicles. With respect to the choice and range of those pictures I have been to a great extent, especially in the first chapter, guided by the light which legends throw upon the dimly-seen period with which they commence, and the often obscure times to which they successively relate ; until that legendary light pales its ineffectual fires at the dawn of the newer day in which Russia, as it were at a bound, due to the mighty impulse given to her course by the creative genius of one who seemed to shape her destiny anew, passed from the obscure seclusion of a semi-Asiatic princedom into the brilliant activity of a vast European empire. It is but a flickering and uncertain light that can be expected to emanate from such traditions as lie embedded in the old chronicles, or such faint echoes of ancient story as have been preserved in the memories of the people : but even its feeble ray often serves as a grateful indication to the explorer who, without its aid, would be in danger of roaming helplessly about the vast and doubtful field which is occupied by early Russian history.

The great Slavonic family, of which the Russian nation is a branch, long ago occupied a considerable portion of Europe; the tide of its migration spreading now here, now there, sometimes flowing unseen in ages too dark for history to illuminate, sometimes visibly following in the wake of Teutonic progress. Vague records of Slavonian barbarism are preserved in Byzantine and other annals, which tell of a people strong and fierce and brave, exceedingly hospitable towards strangers and tolerably tender to domestic slaves, but ferociously cruel in warfare and lamentably indifferent to personal cleanliness; who expected a widow to die on her husband's grave or pyre, and who deemed it the privilege of a mother to slay her superfluous daughters, the duty of a child to provide in a similar way for an aged parent.

But much of this evidence about Slavonic manners, coming from a politically hostile quarter, must be received with that grain of sceptical salt which ought to season the testimony of the ascetic theologians who bear witness against Slavonic heathenism. On the other hand, it is impossible not to regard with some distrust such idyllic pictures of life among the Northern Slavs as have been suggested by the well-known account given of the harpers whom the Greek Emperor Maurice met during one of his expeditions towards the end of the sixth century. They, it is said, were men of noble presence, but who carried musical instruments instead of arms, and who stated that their far-off Northern land could boast of no iron, and therefore weapons were unknown, and men lived a life akin to that led by the blameless Hyperboreans. This legend is probably about as trustworthy as that which tells how, about the beginning of the eighth century, the Khazars—a semi-nomad and seemingly Turkish race—overran the neighbourhood of the Dnieper, and exacted tribute from its Slavonic occupants. Among other things taken from the conquered were swords, but the wiser of the Khazars when they saw them shook their heads, saying:—"The swords of these people have two edges; ours have but one. The time will come when they will conquer us."

Some grain of truth, however, may lurk in the Byzantine tale about the mild and peaceful Arcadians of the North. The "harpers" whom the Emperor met may have been Slavonic minstrels, singers of a nature closely akin to the Celtic bards, the Scandinavian scalds, the Modern-

Greek representatives of the old Hellenic rhapsodists, and all those other laureates of the people who, under divers names, in every quarter of the world, have kept historic memory from rusting, and preserved in song the recollection of days long gone by. For all Slavonic peoples have ever shown themselves lovers of song, and in every Slavonic land there to this day remain some relics of the great mass of popular poetry which, in older times, lauded existing worth and embalmed fond memories of a heroic past. It was probably by such semi-professional singers as these that the metrical romances about Kief and its glories were originally composed and sung—romances which have lately been gathered from the mouths of peasants who, far away on the confines of Siberia, have inherited from a long line of illiterate ancestors such poetic treasures as in more cultured parts of the Russian Empire are utterly unknown.

Very few of the numerous branches of the great Slavonic family now enjoy anything like a vigorous existence. Those of its members who entered what is now North Germany after the Langobardi had swept southwards towards Italy, have in many districts been utterly rooted out, in many others they have been absorbed, only in a few do their descendants prolong a feeble national life—the race which once spread at least as far westwards as the mouth of the Elbe being now represented only by the Kashoubes sprinkled along a part of the coast of the Baltic, and by the Wends of Prussia and Saxony, of whom about 130,000 may still a little longer resist the Germanizing influences which have for centuries been brought to bear upon them. In Bohemia, it is true, wherein a Slavonic tribe replaced the Marcomanni, the Czekhs[1] still hold their own, though with difficulty, against the German and Hungarian contingents of the Austrian Empire; but their survival is due, partly to the mountain bulwark by which their home is environed, partly to the strength of that religious and patriotic enthusiasm which was called into life by the teaching of such national confessors as John Huss and Jerome of Prague, and which so often enabled the inexperienced and scantily-armed followers of Zisca to defy from within the rampart of their chain-linked chariots the seasoned and well-provided soldiery of the German Empire.

Among the other Slavonic subjects of the Emperor Francis Joseph there are but few indications of independent political life. The Slavonians who are or have been exposed to the degrading

[1] With whom the Moravian Slavs may be coupled.

influence of Turkish rule may possibly have a future before them, but at present their position is by no means assured. Poland has been a great power, and might still be of weight in the balance of nations had her nobles been as wise in the senate as they were gallant in the field ; but now she lies prone, pressed to the ground by the joint strength of three mighty empires. At times this Prometheus of nations, driven to madness by the vulture-like gnawing of that "sorrow's crown of sorrow," the remembering happier things, has vainly striven to break the fetters which Force and Might have made secure; but the convulsive efforts of the shackled Titan have proved of but little avail against the disciplined strength of the Imperial Triad into whose hands his liberty has passed.

But there is one branch of the Slavonic family which has not only survived, but has prospered, and has increased. Often was it threatened with extinction during its early career ; for a time it was overwhelmed by the irresistible wave of barbarian conquest. But such vitality did it possess that it rose superior to every disaster, gradually consolidated its strength, and at last throve so vigorously that from being itself attacked it became an attacking, and, in course of time, a widely-subjugating power which can now, like the Andes of the poet, look from its throne "o'er half the world." It is with that branch of the Slavonic family, the core or nucleus of the mighty Russian Empire, that we have now to deal.

The history of the Russian people is to a great extent identified with, or may at least be illustrated by, the history of five cities. These five cities, which are typical of as many periods in Russian history, are Novgorod, Kief, Vladimir, Moscow, and St. Petersburg. Novgorod represents the municipal form of government, such as it existed among the Slavs before a dynasty of foreign extraction became strong enough to break it down. Kief and Vladimir are the representatives of the Princely-Federal form which prevailed after that epoch up to, and during the greater portion of, the Tartar domination. Moscow is the type of Tsardom, the representative of the period during which the land became consolidated, the power of the minor confederate princes was crushed, and the republican privileges of the ancient municipalities were annihilated. Lastly, St. Petersburg represents the imperial period, that city standing prominently forth as the centre and type of the movement which—initiated by Peter the Great, and steadily kept in view by every succeeding monarch—has enabled Russia to develope into the conquering and absorbing power which seems to many eyes to throw so vast and ominous a shadow over Western Europe.

Rather more than a thousand years ago but a small part of the country now called Russia was occupied by what was destined to become its dominant race. But the positions which they held lay along several of the great rivers which constitute the chief nature-boundaries of so level a land. The northern district, of which Lake Ilmen is the central reservoir, was the home of one Slavonic group; westwards another group peopled the basin of the Dvina, and to the south a third occupied the vast extent of country drained by the Dnieper and its affluents. In the centre the upper part of the basin of the Volga, a region of vast and dense forests, was the seat of a number of Slavonic colonies. These constantly came into contact, and frequently into collision, with non-Aryan, chiefly Finnish aborigines, whose prior occupation of so great a portion of Central and Eastern Russia reveals itself in the names of the rivers Moskva, Oka, Kama, and the like, as opposed to the Slavonic names of the western rivers—such as the Boug, in which name may be traced a reference to a once divine being with whom our Bogey was connected before that supernatural creature fell from his high estate, or the Berezina, so called from its groves of *beryozui*, trees known to us by the kindred name of birches.

To these four groups which, as a glance at the map of Russia will show, are linked together by the close proximity of the sources of the chief rivers in their respective fluvial systems, may be added a fourth—that which occupied the basin of the Dniester, a river drawing its waters from a different part of the country from that which gives rise to the other four. The rest of the present empire was the domain of various peoples, settled or nomad, belonging for the most part to the Finnish and Turkish families.

It is to the most northern of these Slavonic groups, located in the regions bordering upon Lake Ilmen, that we will now turn our attention. From immemorial times it was customary for the products of the East to pass westwards through the country which is now called Russia. After reaching and traversing the Caspian Sea they proceeded up the Volga, and then, after a short land journey, they were again placed in boats which brought them to the locality on which—at a time which cannot be fixed with certainty—sprang up the city of Novgorod. This city, as some historians hold, was the centre of a Slavonic federation long before the Varangians, who afterwards became supreme in Russia, had gained any hold on the country. And its position enabled it to thrive rapidly and flourish greatly, acting as an important commercial link between the East and West, communicating with the Baltic by means of the Volkhof which runs into Lake Ladoga, and the Neva which runs out of that lake into the Gulf of Finland; communicating also easily with the Dnieper, and by means of that river with the Black Sea, Byzantium, and the Mediterranean. Over the early history of the Lake Ilmen Slavo-Finnish confederation there broods a darkness dense and hard to be dispelled. Let us avail ourselves then of legendary light, in order to obtain some view, however imperfect, of the onward march of events.

If we look back a little more than 1000 years, we see the Slavonians along the Dnieper paying tribute to the Khazars—that semi-nomad people, apparently of Turkish descent, who occupy all the south of what is now Russia in Europe. And in like manner we find their kinsmen the Northern Slavonians exposed to the frequent ravages, or at least yielding to the influence, of some of the Scandinavian Northmen, who in those days laid under contribution so many widely-separated lands. Later on we see the Slavo-Finnish confederation of the Ilmen district free itself from this foreign influence, pressure, or yoke. But soon afterwards its members find that complete independence is not —at all events to Slavo-Finnish minds—an unalloyed delight. And therefore they begin to allow their memories to dwell with fond regret on the alien but majestic guiders of their by-gone days.

While they are in this melting mood, Gostomysl, Prince or President of Novgorod, feels that his days are drawing to a close. He sees that the commonwealth is threatened with great perils, on account of its constant dissensions and revolutions, and so he calls the people together and beseeches them to invite from abroad some wise and strong man to govern them. And they listen to his voice and send envoys across the sea to the Varangian tribe or family of Rus. The envoys arrive and say, "Our land is large and rich; but order in it there is none. Do ye come over and govern us." And the chieftains of the tribe, Rurik and his brothers Sinëus and Truvor, accept the offer, summon their kinsmen and the rest of the tribe of Rus, and in the year 862 arrive in the land which is thenceforward called *Russkaya,* Russish, or Russian. At first the three brothers occupy separate strongholds, but after two years Sinëus and Truvor die, and Rurik settles and rules supreme at Novgorod.

About this time two of the chieftains among his followers, Ascold and Dir, obtain leave from him to go with their followers to Constantinople, saying that they intend to enrol themselves among the Emperor's Varangian Guards. On their way southwards, as they sail down the Dnieper, they come to a hill-side town. This town, they are told, was founded long ago by three brothers, (after one of whom, named Ky, it is called Kief,) whose descendants now occupy it as tributaries of the neighbouring Khozars. And the place finds favour in the eyes of Ascold and Dir, who settle there, collect around them a number of Varangians, and become the rulers of the whole surrounding district. Before long they think themselves strong enough to undertake an expedition against Constantinople. It fails, being foiled by a tempest which the Greeks attribute to a miracle, and which, men say, affects the minds of Ascold and Dir so strongly that they send to the Emperor for a religious teacher, and accept Christianity at the hands of the bishop who comes to instruct them. And so a Christian temple arises at Kief, crowning those heights on which, as legends tell, St. Andrew the Apostle himself, in the early morn of Christianity, first set up the Cross.

Meanwhile Rurik has been ruling supreme in Novgorod. After a time, it is true, the Ilmen Slavs become discontented, and under a popular leader, named Vadim, they take up arms and would fain free themselves from their Varangian friends. But Rurik slays Vadim, crushes the power of the rebels in his iron grasp, and rules on tranquilly until his death. It is in the year 879 that he dies.

He leaves an infant son, Igor. But the reins of power pass into the hands of his kinsman Oleg, who acts (as some say) as guardian of the child, or who inherits the sceptre (as say others) according to the old Slavonian rule by which a chieftain's brother, or other member of the elder branch, inherits before that chieftain's son.

For three and thirty years Oleg governs the land with wisdom and with power, bringing various Slavonic tribes under his rule, waging war with divers alien peoples, and carrying out almost every enterprise he undertakes. Soon after his accession to power he collects a strong force, and leads it southwards. First he seizes Smolensk, then he drops down the Dnieper to Kief. But before arriving at that city he stays the progress of the greater part of his flotilla, and proceeds with but a few gallies.

to which a commercial air is given, the fighting men being hidden away. Ascold and Dir are invited to visit the ships, in which peaceful merchants are supposed to be making their way towards Greece. They accept the invitation, and go on board Oleg's vessel. But as soon as they are in his power he gives a signal to his warriors, who rush forth from their hiding-place, and seize the unsuspecting chieftains. And Oleg cries:—"Ye are no princes, nor of the princely race ; but I am of the princely race, and here "—pointing to the young Igor—" is Rurik's son," and orders Ascold and Dir to be put to death.

After this Oleg takes possession of Kief—"fit mother of Russian cities," as he calls her—and there fixes his abode. Thenceforward for many a year is Kief the capital of the Russian land.

After rendering tributary various neighbouring Slavonic tribes, Oleg leads a fleet of 2000 gallies against Constantinople, safely passes the dangerous cataracts of the Dnieper, and appears before the Imperial City. Dragging his ships ashore, and mounting them upon wheels, he is even said to have sailed on dry land up to its walls. The terrified Emperor consents to a peace, highly advantageous to the Russo-Varangian invaders. With all solemnity and state he swears to observe it on the Gospels ; they swear by their arms, and by the Slavonic gods

Perun and Volos. Then Oleg nails his buckler to the city gates, and in triumph returns to Kief, where his admiring subjects confer on him the title of *Veshchy*, the Divining, the Seer or Diviner.

Strange to say his disbelief in divination brings about, as legends tell, his end. A warlock tells him that his death will be caused by his favourite horse, whereupon Oleg orders it to be brought out for him no more, but to be carefully provided for. At the end of several years he learns that it is dead, and goes to see its remains. And when he reaches the spot where they lie, he laughs at the unfulfilled prophecy, and sets his foot upon his dead steed's skull. Then from within the skull glides forth a serpent, which stings Oleg in the foot, and of that wound he dies.

On Oleg's death, in 912, the power passes into the hands of Igor, Rurik's son. Like Oleg he rules for about three and thirty years, but he scarcely equals Oleg, either in wisdom or in success. He wages war with the Greeks, but his gallies are consumed with Greek fire, and his land forces, utterly routed, with difficulty make their way back to Kief. A second time he sets out against Constantinople, and on this occasion the Emperor consents to purchase peace with gold, and a new treaty is drawn up between his empire and the country now for the first time officially designated as "the Russian land." When the time comes to confirm the treaty at Kief, we see Igor mount the sacred hill whereon stands the statue of Perun, Lord of the Thunder. There he and his heathen captains lay down their swords and shields and gold therewith, and thus swear to observe their compact. But those among the Varangians who are Christians we see congregating in their church dedicated to Elijah the Prophet, and there on the Gospels taking their oath.

Time passes by: the autumn of 945 arrives. Then Igor's followers call upon him to levy tribute for their benefit, crying, "We are poor and bare; while the followers of the chieftain Sveneld are rich in arms and raiment." So Igor, against his will, sets out on one of the tribute-levying expeditions in which he is wont (as will be his successors after him) to spend the winter of each year. Now among his Slavonic tributaries, the Drevlians, or forest men, are a fiercer race than the Polanians or men of the plain, by whose territory they are divided from Kief. On these Drevlians Igor lays a heavy tax. Not contented with that, he a second time demands money from them. They take counsel together and say: "When a wolf attacks sheep, if he be not killed he will destroy the whole flock. And likewise if we do not kill this man, he will destroy us utterly." Then they send a message unto Igor, saying: "Wherefore comest thou back? Hast not thou received the whole tribute?" But he pays no heed to their words; so they take up arms, and slay Igor and all who are with him.

Now Igor has left a widow, Olga by name. Some writers say that she was a descendant of Gostomysl, that ruler of Novgorod by whose advice the Varangians were first called in. Others assert that she was simply a village maiden, of Varangian descent, whose youthful beauty had smitten the fancy of the young Igor, as he followed the chase one day in the neighbourhood of Pskof. However this may be she was a woman born to command, and we see her throw herself with all the energy of her character into a scheme for revenging her husband's death.

Before long envoys arrive at her palace, sent by the Drevlians to apologize for their having killed her former lord, and suggesting that she should obtain a new one by marrying their prince, Mal by name. Olga feigns acquiescence, and tells the envoys to return next morning, borne aloft in their galley on the shoulders of her subjects. So on the following day they appear, carried along triumphantly in the vessel which has brought them to Kief. But during the night Olga has caused a deep trench to be dug, and into it the galley and its occupants are cast. Then earth is flung in from above, until the envoys are buried alive. And while the operation is going on Olga draws nigh to the edge of the trench, and asks the victims if the honour paid them is to their liking; and they reply, "Our fate is worse than Igor's death." After this Olga summons a fresh set of envoys from the Drevlian land, comprising the noblest of its men of rank. When they arrive, ignorant of what has taken place, she induces them to enter a bath house which has been prepared for their reception; and when they are within its walls the doors are locked, the house is set on fire, and they are burnt to death. Again Olga sends a message to the unsuspecting Drevlians, ordering them to make preparations for a *trizna* or funeral feast to be held above the grave of her dead lord. They obey, and presently Olga arrives, laments in fitting fashion beside Igor's tomb, raises a great *kurgan* or tumulus above it, and then persuades the Drevlians to drink deeply in his honour. And when they have drunk themselves into helplessness, Olga's warriors fall upon them, and slay them to the number of five thousand, after which she returns to Kief.

Somewhat solaced, but not yet satisfied, Olga sets out again next year to punish the Drevlians, drives their forces before her, and lays siege to Korosten, that city of theirs in which Igor was slain. The summer passes by, but the city still holds out. At last Olga grows weary of waiting, and resorts to a new artifice. She sends a message to the besieged, saying that she will spare their city if they will pay her tribute; and the tribute she claims is a leash of pigeons and as many sparrows from each homestead. The birds are gladly sent, but when Olga receives them she distributes them among her troops, who are told to fasten to each bird rags steeped in oil. And at night the rags are set on fire, and then the birds are let loose. In their fright they fly straight to their former homes in the pigeon house or under the thatch. In a few minutes the whole city is in a blaze, and its panic-stricken inhabitants, attempting to escape from a fiery death, fall an easy prey to the swords of the men of Kief. 945 - 957

Having thus fulfilled the sacred duties of a widow, Olga goes back to Kief and turns her attention to her functions as a sovereign. For Sviatoslaf, the son whom she has borne to Igor, is as yet too young to rule. For twelve years does she govern the state, firmly and with wisdom. Then Sviatoslaf succeeds to the throne, and his mother sets out on a journey to Constantinople. There so deep an impression is made upon her by the beauty of the churches and the grandeur of the religious services, that she becomes a convert to Christianity. At the end of her visit she is solemnly received into the Church, the Emperor acting as her sponsor, the Patriarch celebrating the baptismal rite, and dismissing her with the words: "Blessed art thou amongst Russian women, in that thou hast left the darkness, and hast loved the light. Therefore from generation unto generation shall the Russian people call thee blessed."

On her return to Kief Olga would fain induce her son Sviatoslaf to follow her example and adopt Christianity, but that fierce warrior, his whole heart set upon battle and conquest, heeds neither her arguments nor her entreaties, pleading that if he does so his followers will laugh him to scorn. But although he does not share his mother's religious convictions, he holds her wisdom in high esteem, and during the long absences to which his constant wars condemn him, he confides to her the internal administration of the realm.

These wars Sviatoslaf carries on with but varying success, keen-eyed captain and fiery soldier that he is. During one of them, while he is absent from Kief, we see the city all but torn from him by barbaric hands. The Petchenegians, one of the nomad peoples occupying the vast plain sweeping eastward from the Dnieper, foes as terrible to the nascent power of Russia as their predecessors the Khazars had been, besiege the capital and reduce it to the verge of despair. On the farther bank of the Dnieper is stationed a strong Russian force, but its commander does not know to what straits the city has been reduced, and for a long time no messenger is able to reach him. At last a bold youth leaves the city, holding a bridle in his hand. Accosting in their own tongue the Petchenegians whom he meets, he asks them if they have seen his runaway horse. Taking him for one of themselves they allow him to pass through their lines to the river, into which he plunges, swims across to the other side under a shower of arrows, and makes the Russian general acquainted with the desperate condition of the city. The next day Kief is relieved, and soon afterwards Sviatoslaf returns, and drives the Petchenegians far away into the Steppe.

On another occasion we see Sviatoslaf on the point of deserting the banks of the Dnieper with the view of fixing his abode on those of the Danube. At the request of the Greek Emperor he has overrun the land of the Bulgarians, bordering on that river, and now he longs to shift his palace from Kief to their capital, Pereyaslavets, whither (he says) all good things will flow in upon him; gold and silk, and wine from Greece, and silver and horses from Hungary and Bohemia, and from Russia furs and wax and honey and slaves. But when he tells his mother of his project, she pleads that she is now old and feeble, and begs him at least to wait until he shall have laid her body in the grave.

Three days later she dies. And she is buried among the lamentations of the people, who give to her the title of "The Wise," while the Church bestows upon her that of "The Sainted." For many and many a year to come will her subjects, and their children and children's children after them, keep alive the memory of the progresses she was accustomed to make throughout her dominions, collecting taxes and dispensing justice. Centuries hence will her halting-places be shown in many a town and hamlet along the banks of the Dnieper or the rivers of the Novgorod region; while in Pskof, her reputed birthplace, her fellow-citizens will preserve with jealous care the sledge in which the sainted princess was wont to drive.

Soon after Olga's death, Sviatoslaf returns to

Bulgaria, on the Danube; but its inhabitants rise up against him, and this time they are supported by the Greeks. A series of terrible fights ensues. Sviatoslaf and his chieftains perform prodigies of valour, but fate is against them, and after a time they are besieged by an overwhelming force within the walls of Dorostol, the modern Silistria. At last, however, a treaty is concluded between the contending powers, after which an interview takes place between the Greek Emperor and the Russian Prince. It is a striking picture which the annalist has drawn. On the bank of the Danube sits the Emperor John Zimisces on horseback, surrounded by a splendid group of guards. Presently appears Sviatoslaf, rowing himself in a boat. A true warrior chief of the Viking stamp; broad-chested, thick-necked, blue-eyed, with shaggy eyebrows and long moustaches and a light beard, with a ring bearing two pearls and a ruby in one of his ears, and with his head shorn of all but one long lock of hair. The Emperor alights from his horse, Sviatoslaf sits down in his boat, and a conversation ensues between the soldier-chieftains, who part for the time good friends. Never before have Zimisces and Sviatoslaf met, but once before has the Emperor formed a favourable opinion of his Russian foe. In Nestor's narrative we read how Zimisces tests

Sviatoslaf by sending him two kinds of presents: first gold and sumptuous apparel, and then a sword and other weapons. The precious metal and costly raiment Sviatoslaf receives with disdain. But as soon as he sees the weapons he bursts into such a rapture as, like that of the disguised Achilles among the daughters of Lycomedes, reveals his true nature, and renders the Emperor anxious to be on good terms with a prince who shows so haughty a contempt for gold, so genuine a taste for steel.

From Dorostol, Sviatoslaf sails down the Danube, across the Black Sea, and up the Dnieper as high as its cataracts. There he finds the way barred by the Petchenegians, to whom the Bulgarians have sent word that he is coming with much treasure and but a small guard. He tarries below the cataracts; passes the winter there, enduring great distress. At length he attacks the foe, but unsuccessfully. A few only of his followers escape to Kief. Sviatoslaf himself falls. His head is cut off, and his skull, set in gold, serves as a drinking cup for the Petchenegian chief, who causes this device to be carved upon its rim: " In striving for what belonged to others, thou hast lost what was thine own."

It is in the year 972 that Sviatoslaf falls. Some little time before, when about to start on his fatal

Bulgarian expedition, he has divided his Russian domains among his three young sons; giving Kief to Yaropolk, and the Drevlian land to Oleg, and Novgorod to Vladimir. So after their father's death, these three princes rule, each in his own territory. Before long they are literally at daggers drawn. Oleg, as devoted to the chase as our first Norman kings, slays a trespasser on his preserves. The father of the murdered man is Sveneld, the bravest of Sviatoslaf's warriors, and he, thirsting for revenge, induces Yaropolk to attack his brother Oleg. A battle takes place. Oleg is defeated. He flies to the town of Obrutch. Across a bridge outside its gates is streaming a throng of fugitives. Oleg attempts to cross it. Thrust off by the rush of his own flying troops, he falls into a deep moat, and in it is crushed to death beneath a mass of men and horses. It is long before his body can be found, but at last it is drawn from the moat and laid out with all respect. And when Yaropolk sees it he weeps bitterly. He is but a youth of sixteen, and his dead brother was a year younger.

When Vladimir hears the news, fear comes upon him; and he flies from Novgorod, and takes refuge among his Varangian kinsmen. So for a time Yaropolk rules supreme. But at the end of two years Vladimir returns to Novgorod, and recovers his rights. At this time Polotsk, on the Dvina, is ruled by a Varangian chief named Rogvolod, whose daughter Rognéda is betrothed to Yaropolk. Vladimir, who is about to make war on his brother, determines to rob that brother of his bride, and sends Rognéda a proposal of marriage. The haughty maiden replies that she has no wish to marry the son of a slave; to unboot him, says the legend, a Slavonic bride being accustomed, as part of the civil marriage ceremony, to draw off the boots of her lord and master, a custom still kept up among the people. Now Vladimir's mother was Malusha, formerly one of Olga's waiting maids, and therefore a slave; for in those days the acceptance of a menial office is said to have rendered even a free-born person a slave. Stung by this taunt, Vladimir, the slave's son, attacks Polotsk; takes it by storm, slays Rogvolod together with his two sons, and compels Rognéda to marry him.

A marriage so brought about is not likely to prove a happy one. Let us anticipate the course of events, and at once witness its results. A few years have passed. Vladimir, still a heathen, has taken to himself other wives, and the deserted Rognéda determines to be revenged. One day, as Vladimir is lying on his couch asleep, she steals to his side, and is on the point of plunging a dagger into his breast, when he suddenly awakes, and surprises her with arm raised up to strike. When charged with the intended crime, she makes no attempt to deny or palliate her guilt; merely stating that she meant to avenge the slaughter of her kinsmen, and to punish her lord for slighting her. Vladimir resolves to put her to death with his own hand; but first he orders her to array herself in the garments which she wore upon her wedding day, and then to await his approach. She obeys, but meantime she instructs the young son whom she has borne him how to act. So when Vladimir enters the room in which she is to die, his little son meets him, and offering him a drawn sword, says: "Dost thou think that thou art here alone?"

And when Vladimir sees the boy and hears his words, he flings away the sword and leaves the room. Calling together his nobles and councillors, he tells them all the tale, and asks them what he ought to do. They counsel him to pardon the guilty mother for the sake of the innocent child. And Vladimir gives heed to their words, and forgives Rognéda—Gorislava, as the people call her on account of her many sorrows, for *gore* is an old Slavonic word for woe.

After his ill-omened marriage with Rognéda, Vladimir marches against his brother Yaropolk, and besieges him in the town of Rodnia. So great are the sufferings of the besieged that for centuries to come the common people will talk of "Misery like that in Rodnia." At last a traitor induces Yaropolk to place himself within Vladimir's power. We see him cross the threshold of the room in which he expects to find his brother. We see the two Varangians posted behind the door plunge their swords into the body of the youthful prince. He falls, and Vladimir has no longer a brother who may play the part of a rival near his throne.

Some legends assert that Yaropolk had evinced a leaning towards Christianity, and that therefore Vladimir was anxious to exhibit himself in the light of a champion of heathenism. Or it may be that, rendered uneasy by remorse for his brother's death, he strove to propitiate the gods of his idolatry by more than usual zeal for their worship. However this may be, we see him, as supreme chief of the Russian land, setting up fresh idols at Kief, or at least adorning anew those which already stand there.

Now it happens, after a time, that he returns to Kief from a victorious expedition against a neighbouring tribe, and gratefully determines to offer up a human victim to his stern gods. So lots are cast to decide who shall be sacrificed, and their decree selects the son of a certain Varangian who is a Christian. To the dwelling of this Varangian go the representatives of the people, and demand from him his son. But he replies:

"Your gods are no gods, but mere wood: to-day they are, to-morrow they perish: they eat not, neither do they drink, nor do they speak, being made out of wood by man's hands. He alone is God before whom the Greeks bow down and worship. He who made the heavens and the earth, the sun, the moon, and the stars; who created man, and gave him to live upon the earth. But these gods of yours—what have they created? They are themselves the work of others. I will not give up my son unto devils!"

When these words are made known to the people they wax wroth, and break into uproar, and storm the abode of that Varangian, and put both him and his son to death. So perish the first Christian martyrs in the Russian land—martyrs whom to the present day the Church honours under the names of the Holy Fedor and Ivan.

This seeming triumph of heathenism proves to be merely the forerunner of its fall. Soon after its occurrence Vladimir's religious opinions grow unsettled, and he shows a disposition to adopt some other **creed** than that bequeathed him by his Scandinavian and Slavonic forefathers. We see him at first lending ear to Mohammedan proselytizers, finding their glowing descriptions of Paradise much to his taste. But when they tell him that he must give up eating pork and drinking wine, he cries aloud: "We Russians delight in drinking. Impossible for us to live without that." And he thinks no more of the Koran.

Next he listens with favour to what Jewish pleaders urge in behalf of their creed—until it occurs to him to ask where lies their native land. But when they reply that for their sins God has driven them from their own country, and scattered them abroad among the nations, he at once refuses to have anything more to do with so sinful and ill-omened a race.

Then comes a Christian sage. He troubles Vladimir's mind by strange words concerning this life and that which is to come, and confirms the deep impression they have made by revealing to his gaze a pictured scroll on which are represented the souls of the just, angel-led, rising on the right hand into Paradise, and the souls of the unjust, demon-driven, descending on the left into the jaws of hell. Long does Vladimir gaze upon the picture. Then he sighs deeply, and utters words betraying a strong inclination to place reliance upon his new teacher. But before coming to a decision upon so momentous a question he sends envoys into various lands to report upon their respective religions. They, on their return, speak unfavourably of all that they have seen elsewhere, but in rapturous terms do they describe the magnificent rites of the Greek Church, the splendid Christian temples of Constantinople.

Vladimir calls his chieftains together to hear the report of the envoys. And when they have heard it, and they are asked if they are in favour of adopting the religion of the Greeks, they promptly answer "Yes!" adding : " Were it not a good one, would thy grandmother Olga have adopted it—she, the wisest among the children of men ?" Thereupon Vladimir asks: "In what place shall we receive baptism ?" To which their ready reply is, " Wheresoever it pleaseth thee."

Then Vladimir sets out with a great force, sails to the Crimea, and there seizes the Greek city called Korsun, or Chersonesus, near the present Sevastopol. Thence he sends a message to the Greek Emperors Basil and Constantine, demanding the hand of their sister, (or cousin, as some say,) the Princess Anna. They reply that they cannot give their sister to a heathen suitor. Vladimir sends back word that he is ready to become a Christian.

D

On this they yield, but at first the Princess will not consent to marry a barbarian. At last, however, she also gives way, and sets sail to seek her uncivilized wooer, but with a heavy heart, and exclaiming, "I go as though into captivity. Better were it for me to be dying here."

She reaches Korsun, Vladimir is baptized, the marriage is solemnized, and soon afterwards the royal bridegroom and bride arrive at Kief. There Vladimir's own family and his kinsfolk are baptized, and then he orders the idols which he has hitherto worshipped to be destroyed. High on the hill above the river stands a statue of Perun—the Slavonic Thor, the Vedic Parjanya, Lord of the Rain Cloud and the Thunderbolt—his trunk of wood, his head of silver with moustaches of gold. And near it stand the sacred figures of the other deities, under whose forms the heathen Slavonians have personified the forces of Nature—Dazhbog, the Day-God or the Sun, Stribog, god of the winds, and many another time-honoured divinity of old religion. All these hewn and carved images we see, at Vladimir's command, cast down from their high estate. Without a voice being raised in their behalf, some are hacked to pieces, and some are burnt. But the statue of Perun is dragged at a horse's tail down the steep bank to the Dnieper's shore, and there cast into its waves. And on the morning of the next day the people are gathered together, and at Vladimir's command they wade into the Dnieper's stream, and the Greek prelates who have accompanied their Princess from Constantinople offer up prayers and chant psalms, and then receive into the Christian Church the masses of men and women, and children, who stand in the river before them.[2]

From this time forward Vladimir shows himself as zealous for his Christian faith as he has hitherto been for the religion of his heathen ancestors. He builds one church at Kief on the spot where the statue of Perun stood so long, and another on the site of the house in which the two Christian martyrs perished five years before. A little later most of his subjects in the other parts of the land follow the example of the citizens of Kief, and before long Russia becomes a Christian country. In remote districts, it is true, and every here and there amid swamps and forests, the ancient rites are long kept up, the memories of the old religion are long preserved. But in the towns, after a while, Christian churches begin to appear, the Slavonic translation of the Scriptures made by Cyril and Methodius in the ninth century is introduced and

[2] A.D. 988.

disseminated, and schools are opened—to which, however, we see recently converted mothers strongly objecting to send their children, under the impression that reading and writing are manifest inventions of the Evil One.

Devoted to religious observances and the practice of charity, Vladimir becomes so soft of heart that for a long time he refuses to put to death the offenders called " brigands"—in whom some eyes may see stubborn adherents to heathenism. And when the prelates of his church remonstrate with him on his culpable laxity, he replies, " I am afraid of sinning," and with great reluctance yields to their demand for severe measures.

But in spite of his religious fervour he does not forget what he owes to his martial followers, or neglect his duties as a military chieftain. One day when the guests at one of his numerous feasts are excited by their copious draughts of mead, they complain of his meanness in supplying them with spoons made of wood. When Vladimir hears of this he causes silver spoons to be made, saying: " Neither with silver nor with gold can I procure me a warrior band. But these, my warriors, bring me in both silver and gold."

In the field he leads his troops to a series of successes, finally subduing a number of tribes to the north and east, and crushing into comparative insignificance the once terrible hordes of the Petchenegians. It is to one of his campaigns against these wild nomads that a legend is referred, which is very dear to the Russian mind.

A gigantic Petchenegian has challenged the Russian warriors to find him an antagonist. None of Vladimir's heroes venture to meet so terrible a foe. At last an old man, three of whose sons are with him in the Russian camp, sends for his youngest son—a mere lad—and the Slavonic David at once offers to fight the Petchenegian Goliath. But Vladimir declares his strength must first be tested. So a fierce bull is let loose upon the stripling, who not only withstands its charge, but tears a handful of flesh from its side. After this he is allowed to defy the giant, who steps forward haughtily, despising his puny foe. But the youth in an instant seizes the Petchenegian in his grasp and crushes him to death. Dismayed by the fall of their champion, the Petchenegians offer but a feeble resistance, and the Russian arms achieve a complete victory.

After a long series of successful struggles against the barbarous inhabitants of the Steppes, Vladimir, in the summer of 1015, is suddenly taken ill, and very soon afterwards he dies. At first an attempt is made, for political reasons, to keep his death from being known. A hole is cut in the floor of the chamber in which he died, and his body, swathed in a cloth, is lowered through the opening, and then conveyed secretly to the cathedral of Kief. But the next day the people find out what has taken place, and they flock in vast crowds to the church, there to weep and wail over their lost chief. And there after a time his body is laid in a marble tomb. For many and many a year to come will the smoke of incense rise, and the chant of psalms resound, above the spot where the remains of the sainted Vladimir rest beside those of his Greek wife.

CHAPTER II.

SUBDIVIDED RUSSIA.

IN the preceding chapter a sketch has been given of the period marked by the birth and infancy of Russian national life. Hastily glancing again over that period we see how a number of kindred but severed tribes, scantily inhabiting districts dotted at large intervals with clusters of hovels, are gradually drawn together by the firm grasp of a succession of alien rulers, and at length compactly united by the kindly influence of a borrowed religion; we mark the rapid rise of a number of towns, each a centre of civilization as well as a stronghold against hostile barbarism; and at length, when the twilight of the heathen period has passed into the daylight of its Christian successor, when the night fogs have risen which have so long brooded over the face of the land, we are able to obtain at least a glimpse of the nascent monarchy which already stretches from the Gulf of Finland to the neighbourhood of the Carpathians, from the confines of Poland and Lithuania to close upon the confluence of the Oka and the Volga.

From the time when the Varangian Princes cross the Baltic to that in which Christianity is established, the reins of power—if our legendary light may be trusted—never fall into feeble hands. Rurik the Conqueror and his kinsman Oleg the Diviner; Igor, Rurik's son, and his widow, Olga the Wise and Holy; Sviatoslaf, Igor's son, the hero of countless fights; and lastly, Vladimir, Sviatoslaf's son, the Civilizer and Christianizer of the Russian land :—all these (according to legendary lore) are rulers worthy of the name, true scions of the race which, from the stormy shores of the north, so long continued to send forth its hardy warriors on forays crowned by victory and conquest.

Four years after Vladimir's death another truly illustrious prince is seen (this time by historic light) ruling at Kief—Yaroslaf the First. Vladimir divided his realm among his numerous sons, the eldest of whom, Sviatopolk, seized upon the capital, and thus commenced a career which made him known among the people by the name of "The Accursed :" his chief crime being the murder of his two brothers Boris and Gleb, princes whom the

Church has enrolled among the ranks of her Saints, and whose memory, as kinsmen who loved each other dearly, was long held in affectionate remembrance by the people—a people doomed to suffer so long and so bitterly on account of jealousy and hatred among princely kinsmen. But after Sviatopolk the Accursed had a third time committed fratricide, another of his brothers, Yaroslaf, attacked him and drove him out of Kief. Sviatoslaf was restored by the Poles, but only for a while. Defeated on the banks of the Alta, close to the spot where he had caused his brother Boris to be murdered, he fled away into the wilderness, ever crying, " Onwards, onwards, we are pursued," until at last, after long and miserable wanderings, he died.

From 1019 to 1054 Yaroslaf ruled at Kief, and during the latter part of that period his power in Russia was supreme. On many a battle-field he was victorious, crushing the strength and putting an end to the incursions of the semi-nomad Petchenegians, many of whom settled on Russian soil and served under Russian banners. But an expedition against Greece, conducted by one of his sons, terminated unsuccessfully; and with it the last chance which the Varangian princes were to have of fulfilling the prophecy said to have been written by an unknown hand underneath the statue of Bellerophon at Constantinople, to the effect that the day would come when the Russians would seize the capital of the Eastern Empire.

But it is upon the internal administration of his realm that Yaroslaf's claim to be entitled a great ruler mainly rests. Many a city did he found : one of which on the Volga still bears his name, while another, called Yourief, after his baptismal name of Yury or George, is now styled by the foreign designation of Dorpat. Many a waste also did he bring under cultivation, many an addition to the Russian dominions was made under his rule. With his Scandinavian kinsmen, and those of his Swedish wife Ingigerd, he maintained a close alliance, productive of many a story to be found in Icelandic poetry. Thus we read of his support of St. Olaf of Norway against our Canute the Great, and of the hospitable reception he and his wife—who at one time was to have married Olaf—gave to that sainted monarch, when (in the words of the Heimskringla Saga [1])—

"King Olaf eastward o'er the sea
To Russia's monarch had to flee."

But most interesting among the stories of his Scandinavian connexions is that which tells how Harald Hardrada, the Norwegian King who fell in

[1] As translated by Mr. Laing.

battle against our Saxon Harold, loved and won Yaroslaf's daughter Elizabeth. In his youth the Norwegian Harald came to Russia and entered into Yaroslaf's service, but afterwards went on to Constantinople, and fought the battle of the Cross against the Infidel in Africa and Sicily. After many adventures, and after scorning (says tradition) the proffered love of the Greek Empress Zoe, he returned to Russia, and there married Yaroslaf's daughter Elizabeth—" who long his secret love had been," according to the Northern Saga-man. On the expedition which ended so fatally at Staɲford Bridge, Elizabeth accompanied her husband as far as our Western Isles, whence she returned to Norway after his death.

Another of Yaroslaf's daughters married Andrew, King of Hungary, and a third, Anne, became Consort of Henry I., King of France. It was probably by her (thinks Gerebtsof) that the famous *Evangclif*, on which the kings of France used to be sworn, was carried to that country. The priests of the Cathedral of Rheims, where it was religiously preserved, did not know in what language it was written, but they attributed to it a vast antiquity. When Peter the Great came to Rheims he was shown this manuscript, written in an unknown tongue. To the surprise of its guardians he exclaimed as soon as he looked at it, "Why that is my own Slavonic," and commenced reading it aloud.

It may be that it was transcribed by Yaroslaf's express direction, for he was able to read, and greatly delighted in Church books. For religion he did much, he founded the first great school in Russia, he fostered the arts and sciences. But above all, he gave the country its first written code of laws, known as the Russkaya Pravda, or Russian Right. This venerable monument of old wisdom and justice, closely connected with the records of Scandinavian and German jurisprudence, will enable all who consult it to dispose of that sweeping charge of Asiatic barbarism which we so often hear levelled against the Russian princes of the olden days.

After the death of Yaroslaf I. there ensued an evil time for Russia, that of the Appanages. He had divided the land among his sons, entreating them in his will to live in brotherly love, and to honour the eldest among them as a father. But they soon fell out, and there arose throughout the realm first dissensions and then civil wars.

At that time the idea prevailed that every descendant of Rurik had a right to an appanage, or separate principality; and that he was independent of all the other princes except the eldest, who ruled at Kief, and bore the title of *Veliky Kniaz*, or Grand Prince. Now in those days the privileges of seniority passed, when a prince died, not to his son, but to his brother, if he had one. So when a Grand Prince died at Kief, leaving brothers as well as sons behind him, he was succeeded—not by a son, who could have taken his father's seat without producing any confusion, but—by the eldest of his surviving brothers. That brother, being already a ruling prince, vacated a principality when he moved to Kief; which principality was occupied by the kinsman next in order of seniority, who in his turn vacated his principality, and so on until the change had gone down all the line.

The consequence of this system was that the country was kept in a state of perpetual disorder. There was constant shifting, and men's minds were never free from disquietude, never had time to benefit by the great blessings of settled order and established rule. Moreover the changes were often brought about unjustly and unexpectedly. Then anger was bred, resulting in countless evils for the land, into which its quarrelling rulers were always introducing Hungarians, or Poles, or barbarian Polovtsi as allies—allies who pillaged and burnt and murdered to their hearts' content.

This is the dreariest period of Russian history, the annals of which are calculated to repel even the most persevering student, so monotonous are their accounts of how a Vseslaf drove an Iziaslaf from Kief, and how Iziaslaf got back his principality by Polish aid, but was again expelled by a Sviatoslaf and a Vsevolod; how a Yaropolk was murdered by an assassin, who fled to a Rurik Rostislavich, and an Oleg Sviatoslavich let loose on his country a flood of barbarians, who swept across a whole province, burning and pillaging the towns and villages, and carrying off their inhabitants into distant captivity.

Now and then a crime of greater than ordinary magnitude stands out conspicuous from this blood-stained page of history; as when we read how David, Prince of Volhynia, induces Sviatopolk, Yaroslaf's grandson, to lay violent hands on Vassilko, Prince of Galich. It is a terrible picture which the old chronicler brings before our eyes. We see Vassilko seized by means of treachery, loaded with chains, and carried away from Kief in a cart by a party of David's followers. They halt in the little town of Bielgorod, and there the captive prince is taken into a room and thrown down upon the floor. He struggles so violently that additional aid has to be called in. **At last** he is overpowered, crushed beneath the weight of his assailants, and then both his eyes are plucked out. In a state of unconsciousness he is placed once more in the cart and driven further on. After a time the men who have charge of him halt in another small town to dine, and a woman is ordered to wash his blood-stained shirt. Having done this she weeps above his body as though over a corpse. But Vassilko is not dead. Gradually his consciousness returns to him, and sitting up he cries: " Wherefore have I been stripped? In that blood-stained shirt I wished to die, and in it to appear before God."

Sometimes, but rarely, a bright spot relieves this gloomy scene, as when the sons of Yaroslaf meet at Vyshegorod, where the relics of Boris and Gleb, the great Vladimir's sainted sons, are translated in solemn state to a new resting-place, the princely brethren bearing the coffin of Boris on their shoulders into the church, and afterwards feasting together in all brotherly friendship.

Another occasion on which an attempt is made to restore union to the reigning family, and peace to the troubled land, is when six of the contending princes meet together at Liubetch in 1097, and declare that henceforward they will live in amity and singleness of heart, and contribute their united efforts towards the protection of the Russian soil.

Having so resolved, and having kissed the cross upon their resolution, they return home, and straightway recommence their former mode of life. At last, however, the gloom which hangs over the whole scene gives way, and, with the accession to the throne[2] of Kief of a worthy successor of Vladimir and Yaroslaf, there dawns a better day for the Russian land.

Yaroslaf's son Vsevolod had married a Greek Princess, the daughter of Constantine Monomachus, and, from his Greek grandfather, Vsevolod's son Vladimir himself received the name of Monomachus. With him the annals of the chroniclers and the memory of the people have associated many a cherished legend. Thus it is told of him that he undertook to avenge the blinded Vassilko, and made war upon Sviatopolk of Kief, who had delivered that unhappy prince into the hands of his tormentors. Sviatopolk would fain have fled from the capital, but the people would not allow him to leave. So he stayed, and the principal citizens, headed by their metropolitan, and attended by Vladimir's stepmother, the widow of his father

---

[2] In old language, to the *stol*—each successive Grand Prince solemnly taking his seat on the *stol* in the Cathedral of Kief. The word *stol* afterwards gave way to *prestol*, which is now used for the imperial or episcopal throne, ect.

Vsevolod, went out in solemn procession to meet Vladimir, and to entreat him to desist from his threatened attack. And Vladimir was touched by the prayers of the head of the Church, and the tears of his father's widow; and like Coriolanus before Rome, he stayed the onward march of his conquering army.

When Sviatopolk died in 1113, the people of Kief sent to Vladimir, inviting him to occupy the vacant throne, and saying, "Come hither, O prince, and take the place held of yore by thy sire and thy grandsire." At first he would not. But after they had shown their passionate longing for him by plundering the houses of all the Jews in the city— whom Sviatopolk had favoured—he could refuse no longer, and so commenced a reign which gave Russia a breathing space of some twelve years.

To this day the regalia of Vladimir Monomachus are preserved at Moscow in the Treasury, and they long played an important part in the coronation of the Russian Tsars. Tradition asserts that they once belonged to Vladimir's grandfather, the Greek Emperor Constantine Monomachus; and that his successor, Alexis Comnenus, sent them to Kief, where, in his name, the Metropolitan of Ephesus crowned Vladimir as Tsar of Russia. This mark of imperial favour was intended, says the legend, to

E

stop the victorious progress of Vladimir, who had already made himself master of Thrace. What is more certain is that Vladimir was, both before and after his accession to supreme power, really victorious in many warlike enterprises. The chief enemies of the country were at that time the Polovtsi, Oriental barbarians who were to the Russians of that day what the Petchenegians had been to their ancestors, what the Tartars became to their descendants. These Vladimir overthrew, in battle again and again, until their power to endanger the safety of the land was brought low. It was just before commencing one of his victorious expeditions against the Polovtsi, while Sviatopolk was still ruling at Kief, that some of that prince's captains objected to commencing hostilities, saying, "It is now the spring: this is not a time for taking the peasant from his plough." But Vladimir replied, "Verily, ye take pity upon the peasant and his horse, and do not bear in mind that while the peasant is ploughing, the Polovtsi will come, and will pierce him with arrows, consume his homestead with fire, and carry off not only his horse, but also his wife and his children." Whereupon they all consented to fight, and a great victory was the result.

No less important than the military exploits

of Vladimir Monomachus were the benefits he conferred on his realm as an administrator. Many a new city sprang into life during his rule, the most important being that which bore his name of (Vladimir) and afterwards became for a time the capital of Russia; and many a city already existing grew and thrived, and waxed strong and secure under his fostering care. But greatest among his peaceful works was the " Code of Laws " which was compiled by his orders, an enlarged recension of that issued by his grandfather Yaroslaf under the name of Russkaya Pravda, or Russian Right. From it and from the testament which he left behind him for the benefit of his children, may be seen how enlightened as a lawgiver, how wise as a prince, how venerable as a house-father, was the ruler of the Russian people during the first quarter of the twelfth century.

One special point of interest for us in Vladimir's life is his marriage, or at least one of his marriages. We have seen how Yaroslaf's daughter Elizabeth attended to our Western Isles her husband, Harald Hardrada, when he joined Toste against our English Harold, and fell at Stamford Bridge. Soon after the widowed Elizabeth had sailed back to Scandinavia, she was followed by the fugitive family of the Harold who conquered at Stamford

Bridge, but was himself conquered and slain at Senlac. According to Icelandic sagas, Gyda, our Harold's daughter—a daughter by Edith of the Swan's Neck, thinks Mr. Freeman—after spending some time in Denmark, was married to a Russian Prince, who seems to have been Vladimir Monomachus. And thus a royal daughter of Saxon England became consort of the ruler of that country from which a prince of ours, bearing the name of the greatest of our Saxon kings, has so recently brought home an imperial bride.

The death of Vladimir Monomachus, in 1125, is followed by a time of terrible disaster for Russia. Heralded by earthquake and eclipse, by famine and by pestilence, there ensues a period of internal disturbance rising at intervals into civil war—a period resembling, but in an aggravated form, that which preceded Vladimir's accession. Again a confused mass of ever-shifting figures occupies the stage; on which from time to time the train of some darker than usual tragedy comes sweeping by. Thus, on one occasion, we see an angry crowd surging around the prison in which are confined the two young nephews of the reigning prince; insisting on the prisoners being deprived of their eyesight, and refusing to depart till the youths are brought forth and shown to them, with pierced eyelids, and with blood-stained cheeks. It is a relief to see that shortly afterwards, the apparently blinded youths recover their sight at the tomb of the Holy Gleb, the special patron of ill-used members of the reigning family, but their fortunate escape from life-long darkness proves unique. On other occasions of a similar kind, the blinders do their horrible work too well.

At another time we see a band of armed conspirators steal in the dead of night into the palace of the Grand Prince Andrew, attack him in his sleep, and leave him to all appearance lifeless. But his wounds are not mortal. He recovers his consciousness, makes his way out of his bedchamber, and staggers along a corridor in search of help. Meantime, his enemies have procured a light, and they return to see if their murderous deed be completed. Finding his bedchamber vacant, they seek him in the corridor, guided by the bloodstains which he has left behind upon the walls and floor, and presently they discover him crouching behind a pillar. This time the assassins make sure of their prey.

On a third occasion we see a dethroned Grand Prince of Kief, Igor by name, living as a monk in the seclusion of a convent. Suddenly, at a moment of national excitement, the people demand the death of him whom they once obeyed. The reigning prince is absent from Kief, but his brother Vladimir attempts to quell the riot, and to rescue its intended victim. All his efforts, all his entreaties, are in vain. For a time the terrified Igor is concealed, but at length the rioters burst into his hiding-place, put him to death, and drag his naked corpse into the market-place. Thence it is conveyed by the Prince's officers into a church, and on the following day it is laid in the grave, arrayed in monastic garb. At the end of the funeral service, the officiating priest turns to the lookers on, and cries, "Woe unto the living! woe unto the stiffnecked and hard of heart!" At this moment a peal of thunder resounds, and the terrified people fling themselves with tears and groans upon the ground.

It is during these evil times that the glory of Kief passes away. The city founded by Ascold and Dir, and fostered by Oleg the Diviner, and by Igor, and by Igor's widow, the wise Olga; the city from which, under the first Vladimir, Christianity poured forth its sunlight over Russia, the city which Yaroslaf the Wise and his grandson, the second Vladimir, surnamed Monomachus, ruled so gloriously; that "mother of Russian cities," as Oleg named her, falls now from her high estate. In the year 1169, during one of the chronic wars among the Princes, a powerful army raised by Andrew, Prince of Souzdal or Vladimir, and commanded by no less than ten princes, assembles on the banks of the Dnieper, attacks Kief, and carries the city by storm. For three days are its palaces, its churches, and the homes of its citizens, given up to pillage. Afterwards it passes into the hands of Andrew's younger brother: but it never recovers from the blow it has received, and from this time forward its rank as the capital of Russia is transferred to younger rivals.

The first of these rivals to assume the title wrested from Kief, is Vladimir, the city founded and named by Vladimir Monomachus, and enlarged and strengthened by the foreseeing care of Andrew Bogoliubsky, the son of the Prince who succeeded to the rule of Kief in 1154. It is this Andrew, Prince of Vladimir (or of Souzdal, as his principality is otherwise called), who storms and pillages Kief in 1169. Holding both cities in his power, he continues to reside at Vladimir, and so to that city is transferred the pre-eminence accorded by custom to the dwelling-place of the reigning Grand Prince. And this pre-eminence is enjoyed by the city called after Vladimir, until she is despoiled of it by her younger sister Moscow.

Soon after the fall of Kief, we see Novgorod attacked by Andrew's victorious troops. But its brave and haughty citizens, proud of an independence of which the men of Kief could not boast, offer a stronger resistance. While they man its walls and defend themselves valiantly against its besiegers, their Archbishop, accompanied by all his clergy, carries in solemn procession to the ramparts the sacred picture of the Blessed Virgin. A hostile arrow strikes the holy icon, whereupon, as legends tell, the Virgin turns her face away from the foe and towards the city, while from her eyes a flood of tears streams over the robes of the Archbishop. A panic seizes the besiegers; a holy indignation nerves the arms of the besieged. The men of Novgorod sally forth, fall headlong upon the enemy, destroy a great part of the Souzdal troops, and take so many prisoners, that "a score of Souzdalers are sold for two pieces of silver." From that time the 27th of November is annually celebrated at Novgorod, as a day to be kept holy, in grateful remembrance of heavenly aid in time of peril. Later on, it is true, we see Novgorod submitting itself to the reigning Prince of Souzdal, Vsevolod, and accepting a ruler at his hands. But later still, we witness the complete discomfiture at Lipetsk of the Souzdal troops, under Vsevolod's son, by the united forces of Novgorod and Smolensk.

And so amid constant changes and ceaseless wars the years go by, and still we see the soil of Russia a prey to endless confusion; the air never free from the dust-clouds raised by troops marching from one part of the land to attack another part, or from the wreaths of smoke rising above towns and villages fired by kindred hands. Of alien enemies also there is no lack. Towards the south-west the Poles and Hungarians are a standing menace, which often passes into an actual peril. Westward also, but more to the north, the Lithuanians, after a long subjugation to the Russians, first become independent, and then attack the frontier provinces of their former lords. Somewhat later, also, the knights of the German Order of the Swordbearers become a power in Livonia which threatens the existence of the neighbouring Russian cities, especially that of Pskof, which is kept in a constant state of alarm. In the north and north-east the Russians have to deal chiefly with less redoubtable foes, the Finnish races never having shown any great power of active resistance;

but, even when defeated, these rude aborigines retard by their presence the civilization of the land. To the south the Polovtsi are no longer the formidable enemies they were before their strength was broken by Vladimir Monomachus, their hordes often being subsidized by the Russian princes with whom their own chieftains are sometimes linked by family ties. Still they occupy in their nomadic style a vast extent of what is now called South Russia, a region from which they might easily be driven if the Russian princes were united.

But those princes, blinded by their own conceit, and deaf to the words of wisdom which, chiefly uttered by the lips of the clergy, strive from time to time to gain their ear, pay no heed to warning sights and sounds until—when rather more than a score of the years of the thirteenth century are spent, some 460 years after the time when Rurik and his Varangians founded the Russian monarchy —a cloud begins to darken ominously in the east, and a voice, at first low and vague, but gradually rising into certainty and strength, tells of a new race of foes, mustering in countless hordes along the south-east frontier of the Russian land. The period of federal-princely Russia is drawing to its close. The time of the Tartar Yoke is nigh at hand.

CHAPTER III.

THE TARTAR INVASION.

IT is in the year 1223 that the Tartars[1] suddenly attack the Polovtsi, that Oriental and partly nomad people which in former days brought so many evils upon the Russian land. Towards the close of his reign Genghis Khan— the monarch of Central Asia who held that as there was but one sun in heaven so there ought to be but one ruler, and that he himself, on earth— wages war against Sultan Mohammed, the ruler of Transoxiana, sweeps like a consuming tempest across his realm, ruins the splendid cities of Bokhara and Samarkand—"those two pearls of great price"—and breaks the heart of their fugitive lord, who dies "so poor and so utterly abandoned,

[1] See p. 198. Throughout this part of the book I use the name by which the invaders are popularly designated.

that for want of a shroud it was necessary to bury him in the only suit of clothes he possessed."[2] A little later the vanguard of the Tartar forces proceed westward, follows the southern shores of the Caspian Sea, turns the flank of the Caucasus, and suddenly appears on this side that mountain bulwark.

The occupants of the plains over which the Tartar cavalry is now sweeping are those Polovtsi with whom the Russians have so often had to fight. But now they fly to Russia for aid against what they call the common foe. The princes of South Russia meet on the Dnieper, and consider what course they shall take. The Polovtsi urge that if they are crushed the Russians will be attacked next. But the Tartars send peaceful messages, declaring that they have no ill-will against the Russians, desiring merely to punish their slaves the Polovtsi. At length the Russian princes determine to support the Polovtsi, break up their camp on the Dnieper, and march eastwards as far as the river Kalka. On the banks of that small river, not far from where the town of Mariùpol now stands, on the flat shores of the Sea of Azof, the Russian and the Tartar forces meet face to face. A battle ensues in which the Russians fight bravely, but, deserted by their allies the Polovtsi, they at length suffer a crushing defeat.

[2] A.D. 1220. Vámbéry's " Bokhara," p. 135.

THE TARTAR INVASION. 61

The Tartars pursue their flying foe right up to the banks of the Dnieper, turning into a desert the land through which they pass. But when they reach the Dnieper they suddenly halt, wheel their countless squadrons, and ride back again to their far-off Asiatic homes.

Some fourteen years pass by, during which no news of the Tartars makes its way to Russia, and gradually the recollection of their invasion fades away like that of some terrible dream. The princes of Russia forget the lesson which has been read them, and recommence their quarrels; or, if they take measures against the enemies of the country, turn their attention exclusively to the Lithuanians and the Finns. Only the common people forebode some coming woe, seeing it predicted by the signs of the times, recognizing omens of ill in meadows parched by drought, and crops withered by blight, in the dense fogs which hide the face of the land, in the plagues which sweep away masses of men and beasts, in the fires which blaze among the forests, and in the burning star of which the brilliant train now sweeps nightly across the sky to trouble nations.

In the year 1237 the Tartars reappear in Russia, under the command of Batu,[3] grandson of Genghis

[3] The Russians write Baty.

Khan, and nephew of the reigning Grand Khan. After subduing the Bulgarians on the Volga, they strike westwards into the principality of Riazan. From its rulers Batu demands tribute. They send for aid to the princes of Northern Russia, but those selfish and short-sighted rulers refuse it, imagining that they will be able to deal with the Tartars independently of their kinsmen. Then the Riazan princes, though all unsupported, fling themselves desperately on the overwhelming Tartar force, but are repelled with terrible loss. Onwards sweep Batu's victorious horsemen, slaying and burning as they go. Before them flies a crowd of homeless fugitives, behind them is left a desolate waste, strewed with dead bodies, and dark with the smoke of burning villages. One after another the Russian cities go down. Riazan, Moscow, Vladimir—all are stormed and sacked, their brave defenders being piteously massacred. On two occasions do the Russian troops make a desperate stand against the foe, but all in vain. Each time their forces are crushed beneath the irresistible weight of the Tartar host. Onwards to the northwest still presses Batu, and Novgorod the Great seems to be doomed to the terrible fate which so many Russian cities have undergone, when suddenly Batu halts—his horsemen being probably impeded by the marshy nature of the soil. The Tartars turn again, as they turned before on the banks of the Dnieper, and after destroying Kozelsk —a town which immortalizes itself by so heroic a defence as gains it from the foe the noble title of "The Evil City"—they return to the Steppes of the Don, where for a time they remain apparently inactive.

But next year—in 1239—they reappear, sweep right across South Russia, and destroy, after a spirited defence, the city of Tchernigof. Next year—in 1240—Batu's forces appear before Kief, and commence the siege of that city. Fallen as it is from its pristine high estate, this ancient capital of Russia can still boast of many charms, of much splendour. Brightly gleam the golden domes of its churches, and shine the walls of its palaces, standing out in clear relief against the sky on the summit of the steep cliffs rising above the Dnieper, girdled by white walls supporting richly decorated towers, and surrounded by groves which far and wide extend their leafy shade. But all these splendours and charms are doomed to disappear. The Tartars invest the city on every side, and thunder against its walls with their battering-rams, until a breach is made, and the outer rampart scaled. Night separates the combatants. The Tartars halt among the ruins till daybreak, and then renew the fight.

Kief falls. Its churches, palaces, and homesteads are consumed with fire; its citizens are slain or led into captivity. Of the ancient capital of the early princes of Russia nothing is left but a heap of smoking ruins. So for a time disappears from history the city with which, of all the cities of ancient Russia, the most glorious historical associations are connected.

From the banks of the Dnieper Batu moves westward into Hungary, Poland, and Moravia, but fortunately for Western Europe he meets, after a time, with a check which induces him to retrace his steps to the Volga, where, rather lower than the present town of Tsaritsyn, he founds what becomes the headquarters of the Golden Horde, the magnificent city of Sarai.[4]

From this time forward, for more than two centuries, Russia is a Tartar province; its people paying tribute, its princes doing homage, to the Tartar Khan. No vast wave of Tartar invasion sweeps across Russia for nearly a century and a half, for the spirit of the country is so completely cowed, and its military force so crushed, that no

[4] *Sarai*, whence Seraglio, means mansion, palace, &c.

important resistance to their power ever obliges the
Tartar monarchs to devastate a land from which
their principal aim is to draw an ample revenue.
But the sufferings of the people endure long after
the invasions which have caused them are over;
and their princes and nobles, during the whole
period of the Tartar yoke, are obliged to submit to
the most degrading humiliations, and to purchase
the right of ruling at home by the most abject
submission abroad.

A vast tract of Russian soil has been turned into
a desert, the few survivors of its former population
having fled into more fortunate districts, or being
detained in harsh captivity by their barbarous
conquerors. Many a year passes away before the
ruined towns and villages can be rebuilt, and the
fields which have relapsed into a wild state can
once more be brought under cultivation. For a
considerable time after the ebbing of the great tide
of destruction which has flowed over the country,
a death-like silence prevails in the devastated land.
The invasion has been, says a Russian writer,[5] like
one of those fires which at times sweep across the
Steppes at the time of the summer heats. Then
a fearful spectacle meets the eye. The thick smoke
creeps along the earth, or rises aloft in spiral folds

[5] Petrushevsky, " Razskazui," p. 64.

until it forms a vast cloud which blots out the sky, and underneath it the advancing fire glows and sparkles and roars. And like the Steppe after the fire has passed, whereon no living being moves, no grass waves in the wind, but all is silent, and waste, and dead, is the face of the Russian land after the Tartar hosts have disappeared. The cities are mere masses of ruins, the villages nothing more than heaps of ashes. The fields lie untilled and overrun with weeds, and all around reigns the stillness of the primeval wilderness, a silence seldom broken by living voice other than the howl of the wolf, and the cry of the bird of prey, except where here and there the few sad survivors from the general wreck weep over the blackened remains of what were once their homes.

Time passes by, and the wounds inflicted by the Tartar invasion slowly heal. But the Tartar yoke continues to press heavily on the shoulders of the Russian people, and the weight of the blow which has crushed their national spirit cannot be shaken off. Poor as are the cultivators of the soil which the Tartars have ravaged, and the citizens of the towns which the Tartars have sacked, they are still obliged to find the means of paying the taxes which their conquerors harshly assess and insolently enforce. Evil tidings are constantly coming to their ears of how their princes have been exposed to insults, sometimes even to torture and death, in the far distant camps of their barbarous masters; and from time to time a terrible rumour spreads abroad that the Tartars are coming back, that their wild horsemen are close at hand, that in a few hours the horrible scenes, at the mere remembrance of which their blood runs cold, will be repeated around their own so lately restored homes. No wonder that at a time when Russia offers so gloomy a picture, the eyes of men should dwell with affectionate reverence on the one figure which seems to be touched by sunlight from on high—that of Alexander, Prince of Novgorod, afterwards known to grateful Russia by the name of St. Alexander Nefsky.

Novgorod had been subject to the Princes of Kief ever since Rurik's successor took up his abode on the banks of the Dnieper; but Kief was far away, and Novgorod was able to maintain a kind of independence. It chose its own princes, exacted from them an oath to respect its constitutional privileges, and sometimes even expelled them when they infringed its rights. Nor did the prince of the day exercise undivided power. The city possessed its own civil and military chiefs whom the prince was bound to consult; and its Vetché, or popular assembly, which might be convoked by any citizen who chose to sound the tocsin, discussed and settled like a free parliament all questions of vital importance. Enriched by the commerce of the East and West, between which they formed a central link, rendered hardy by their frequent contests with their neighbours, and saved, when safety seemed hopeless, from the horrors attendant on Tartar conquest, the people of Novgorod kept alive in Northern Russia that independent and martial spirit which had been almost trampled out in the rest of the country. And, fortunately for them, they possessed, at a most critical time, a prince who was capable of directing that spirit aright.

If we look back a few years from the period at which we have arrived, we shall see that Alexander Yaroslavich has become Prince of Novgorod at the age of seventeen, in the year 1236, just before the second invasion,—that under Batu, the renewal of which proved so fatal to Kief. At this time Novgorod is exposed to great danger from the Swedes, who not contented with forcibly converting the heathen Finns, desire also to bring over the Christian Russians from the Eastern to the Western Church.

It is in the summer of the year 1240, when the Tartars are on their way to Kief, that the Swedish ships enter the Neva, intending no doubt to sail up it into Lake Ladoga, and thence along the Volkhof into the heart of the Novgorod territory.

But Alexander has raised an army in haste, and directly after the invaders have landed, he arrives in the neighbourhood of the spot where, on the banks of the Neva, they have pitched their tents near their ships. Here he is met, traditions tell, by Pelgousy, the chief of the guardians of the coast, an Ingrian Finn, but, unlike the mass of his countrymen, a Christian. And Pelgousy tells Alexander how, as he was watching the shore about sunrise, he heard a sound coming from the sea; and when he looked seawards he saw a bark, at the prow and stern of which sat rowers, their faces hidden as though in mist. But in the centre, clad in purple robes, shone the bright forms of the sainted brothers Boris and Gleb, the martyred sons of the great Vladimir. And Boris said, "Brother Gleb, bid the rowers speed; for it behoveth us to succour our kinsman Alexander, the son of Yaroslaf." Then over Pelgousy came a great fear and trembling, and the bark disappeared from before his eyes.

When Alexander hears these tidings he rejoices

greatly, and prepares for battle with a hopeful heart.

On the 15th of July the Novgorod forces attack the Swedes, utterly rout them, and are prevented only by nightfall from destroying or capturing the whole of their forces. The north of Russia is saved from danger, and its inhabitants in their gratitude to Alexander, and their admiration for the personal valour he has shown, confer on him the honourable title, afterwards ratified by the whole nation, of Nefsky, or "of the Neva."

Soon afterwards, however, the turbulent Novgorodians find fault with Alexander's strict rule, and he becomes wroth and leaves the city. But before long Novgorod is again threatened by a powerful foe; and the city humbles itself before Alexander, who returns, and a second time saves it. This time it is its German neighbours who threaten its existence—the Livonian knights, known as the Sword-bearers, because they bear a red cross on the shoulder of a white mantle, and who have not long before incorporated themselves with the Knights of the Teutonic Order. These dangerous foes essay the feat in which the Swedes have failed, that of converting the Russians at the point of the sword, as they have already converted the Livonians—who, it may be observed, used sometimes, after being baptized, to leap into the Dvina, in the hope that its waters would wash off the effect of the compulsory and unwelcome rite, and bear its traces back to German shores.

The invaders at first carry all before them, seize Pskof, Novgorod's outlying sister city, and advance within a short distance of Novgorod itself. But Alexander having obtained aid from his father Yaroslaf, now Grand Prince of Vladimir, retakes Pskof, and attacks the Germans in their own territory. In the beginning of April, 1242, the opposing forces meet at the junction of the Lakes of Peipus and Pskof, and a hard-fought battle takes place upon the ice. "Judge Thou my cause, O Lord," cries Alexander, as he goes into action. "Aid me as Thou didst aid my ancestor Yaroslaf against Sviatopolk the Accursed." The German troops, with their Tchud allies, form a wedge [6] which bores its way steadily into the Russian line, and seems to be about to cut it asunder, when suddenly Alexander attacks the foe from behind. In a short time the Russians gain a complete victory, and Alexander returns in triumph to Pskof and to Novgorod, where for more than three hundred years afterwards the anniversaries of "The Battle of the Neva," and "The Slaughter on the Ice,"

[6] Known by the technical term of "a pig."

will be celebrated by the Church with solemn memorial services.

A third foe remains to be conquered—Lithuania. Originally tributary to the Russians, the Lithuanians have gradually gathered strength enough to become first independent and then aggressive. But although destined to figure among the most dangerous enemies that Russia will know, they are not at this time able to offer a successful resistance to Alexander. He attacks them upon their invading the Novgorod territory, utterly defeats them, and drives them back into their own land, so broken in spirit that for seven years no news of them makes itself audible to Russian ears.

No wonder that the fame of Alexander of Novgorod spreads far and wide throughout Russia, that towards him the eyes of Russian men should turn wistfully in hopes of aid. Beaten down by the irresistible rush of Tartar invasion, their hearts well-nigh broken by the sufferings they have undergone, their national pride turned to shame and confusion, the inhabitants of Southern Russia recognize some solace in their woe, some mitigation of their disgrace, when they hear how their countrymen in the north have been thrice led to victory over foreign foes by a Prince, to whose side Heaven itself is said to incline. But not to Russia only is his renown confined. The mighty conqueror Batu himself hears of his fame, and desires to see him. So Alexander sets out for Sarai, the headquarters on the Volga of the Golden Horde, and there Batu receives him kindly and with respect, saying to those about him, "What I have heard of this Prince is true; there is none like unto him." After a time Batu sends him on to where, far away in the depths of Asia, dwells the Great Khan himself. And Alexander finds favour in the eyes of that mighty potentate also, the Lord of the Mongol realm which sweeps from the Amoor to the Danube. And the great Khan deigns to confer on him first the rank of Prince of Kief, and afterwards that of Grand Prince of Vladimir, now the capital of Russia.

It is a bright day for the city of Vladimir when Alexander Nefsky enters its gates as its ruler, received in solemn state by the Metropolitan and his clergy, behind whom throng the citizens—full of joy just now at having escaped the horrors of a Tartar siege. For Alexander's predecessor, his brother Andrei, had called down upon the land the wrath of its Tartar masters, who were appeased only by Alexander's prudent submission. With the Tartars, indeed, Alexander has to use other measures than those which he has employed against the German,

Lithuanian, and Swedish foes of Novgorod. Against their overwhelming hosts warlike deeds would be of no avail ; it is only by means of a wise humility that he is able to reason with the master of so many legions.

A few years go by. Batu dies, and his successor decrees that the inhabitants of Russia shall be numbered, with a view to a fresh settlement of taxation—every man having to pay a poll-tax, with the exception of the monks and the secular clergy. This head-tax weighs heavily on the people, the poor having to pay equally with the rich; and Alexander tries hard, but in vain, to induce the Khan to withdraw his orders. Before long arrive the Tartar census-officials, and count and assess the inhabitants of a great part of Russia. Novgorod escapes for a time, but soon come orders from the Khan that Novgorod shall be treated in the same way as the rest of Alexander's dominions. And Alexander himself, who has warded off so many attacks from that city, is obliged to accompany thither the agents of Tartar insolence and greed. Now Novgorod has as yet escaped from Tartar occupation. Her turbulent and haughty citizens know by hearsay only of the horrors of Tartar invasion and conquest, and in their pride they refuse to allow themselves to be numbered and taxed at the will of a distant barbarian. Alexander's entreaties and orders are alike disregarded, and the Tartar emissaries are obliged to retire. Next year he brings them back again, knowing (it is pleaded) that the only chance of saving Russia from the Khan's wrath lies in fulfilling his orders; and he so alarms the leading citizens that they agree to submit. But the common people burst into uproar, sound the tocsin, and hold a tumultuous assembly around their cathedral, crying aloud, " We will die gloriously in defence of St. Sophia and the angelic halls ; we will not be numbered and taxed by accursed feeders on raw flesh." Then Alexander and the census-takers quit the city as though to leave it to its fate. Fear comes on the people. The counsels of the wealthier prevail, and Alexander is entreated to return. From house to house go the Tartar officials, numbering the inhabitants and levying tribute. Then they go back to their master, and Alexander returns to his palace at Vladimir.

After a while the Tartars give up levying the taxes themselves ; farming out the revenue to merchants from Kherasm, the present Khiva. Against these merchants, and against the Baskaks, or Tartar revenue officers, all of whom alike grind down the people and deprive them of their hard-earned gains, the popular indignation grows loud and strong; until at last, driven to despair by intolerable extortions, the inhabitants of a number of towns in Central and Southern Russia simultaneously rebel, assemble hurriedly at the tocsin's call in front of their churches, and slay or expel the foreign tax-gatherers. It is a critical moment for Russia. If the wrath of the Khan is not appeased the Tartars may again descend upon the land, and at one fell swoop annihilate the national life which is struggling so hard to maintain its existence. Alexander sets off at once for Sarai, in order to induce the Khan to overlook what has taken place. He succeeds, and Russia is spared a new invasion. But this is the last service Alexander is able to render his afflicted country. On his way home he is struck down by illness, and on the 14th of November, 1263, clad in monastic robes, and having received the monastic tonsure, he ends a life which has proved of inestimable value to his country.

In the cathedral at Vladimir the Metropolitan Cyril is officiating at the altar when the news of Alexander's death is brought to him. Turning to the people, he cries aloud, "Oh, my children! the sun of the Russian land has set!" And the people answer with a wailing cry, "We are lost!" A few days later-the corpse of their late prince is brought to Vladimir. A terrible frost has set in, but in spite of that the whole city, small and great, goes out some four miles to meet the body of him whom living they have loved so well. In the monastery of Vladimir his remains are laid with sad solemnity, and there they rest until, between four and five centuries later, Peter the Great transports them to St. Petersburg, where, on the banks of the river from which he derives his popular designation, reposes all that is mortal of Saint Alexander Nefsky.

The wisdom of Alexander Nefsky proved of the highest service to Russia. But there was another element in the moral force which held together and ultimately saved the realm, when it was reeling beneath the crushing blows of its gigantic antagonist. That element was supplied by the Church. At a later period we shall see how greatly such men as St. Alexis and St. Sergius helped to maintain that concord among the Russian princes without which Russia could never have been freed. But even now, during the darkest period of Russian history, we can discern the priceless services rendered by the Russian Church to the Russian land.

It was the Church which sustained the courage of the Russian people during the agony of the Tartar invasion, which comforted the countless mourners over the dead, which took away its sting from death itself for those who were doomed to die.

Enter any country church in Russia—not some gorgeous cathedral conveying the idea of a church triumphant, but some humble edifice, plain as a meeting-house in many of its details—and watch the rustic congregation at their devotions. Study the expression, pleading or grateful, which softens or enlivens so many ordinarily dull and stolid faces. And then, as you think of all that these poor peasants have gone through, of all that their ancestors have suffered, you will be able to realize to some extent what the Church was for Russia during the terrible time of the Tartar invasions.

And again, pass through some Russian village after nightfall, and mark, amid the darkness, the tiny spark which gleams through one of the windows of every house. That spark burns in the lamp which hangs before the icon, the holy picture, the central point of the Russian homestead. In it we, knowing what Russia has been, may be allowed to see a type of the kindly light which the almost heart-broken people of devastated Russia saw gleaming from amid the surrounding gloom—light which, though dim and fitful, was for them the presage of a coming dayspring from on high ; light which for them, almost whelmed beneath the wave of Mongol barbarism, kept before their eyes the form of Him who of old, when the bark of His disciples seemed to be foundering in the Lake of Gennesaret, "rebuked the wind and the raging of the water ; and they ceased, and there was a calm."

CHAPTER IV.

THE TARTAR YOKE.

IN the three preceding chapters I have attempted to give a sketch of Russian history, first during its legendary period, up to the introduction of Christianity under Vladimir the First—then during the troublous times in which its disunited principalities were perpetually at variance—and lastly, during the disastrous years which witnessed the first two Tartar invasions, and the commencement of the Tartar domination. The space of time over which our eyes have glanced comprises just four centuries. About the year 862 we saw Rurik and his Varangian followers, natives of a vague Scandinavian district, occupy the country between Lake Ladoga and Lake Ilmen, and soon afterwards we witnessed the foundation of the Principality of Kief, the conversion of its inhabitants to Christianity, and the rapid spread of the realm of which it formed the most important province. In 1015, and again in 1054, and a third time in 1125, we saw the land rent in pieces on the death of a St. Vladimir, a Yaroslaf the Wise, and a Vladimir Monomachus; and we were dimly aware of a prolonged confusion lasting until, during the first half of the 13th century, the Tartars swept across the country like a destroying torrent, and Russia became a tributary province of the Mongol Empire. With the death of Alexander Nefsky, in the year 1263, our survey comes to a close.

As the glories of the old city of Kief, the first capital of ancient Russia, are associated in legendary lore with those of St. Vladimir, her first Christian prince, so is the memory of the city of Vladimir, the supplanter of Kief as the capital of the land, closely connected with that of St. Alexander Nefsky. But the fortunes of the city to which we are now about to turn our attention, the city which supplanted Vladimir, as Vladimir had supplanted Kief, are linked with those of a series of princes, many of whom were remarkable for worldly wisdom rather than for saintly virtues. That city is Moscow. In the next chapter I propose to describe at greater length its rapid growth, and the swift strides towards pre-eminence of the principality to which it gave its name. At present we will merely glance at its early history, in order not to distract our attention from the general picture of the Tartar occupation of Russia.

About a hundred years before the first Tartar invasion, a certain noble, Stepan Kuchko by name, possessed a village which stood on a hill rising above the river Moskva. This village was called after its proprietor Kuchkovo. The Grand Prince George, son of Vladimir Monomachus, happening to pass that way, and being averse to Kuchko, put him to death, and ordered a small wooden town to be built upon the site of his village. To this town he gave the name of Moskva (our Moscow), derived from the river which it overlooked—a name which does not appear in the chronicles earlier than the year 1147.

Up to and for some time after the second Tartar invasion—that under Batu—during which it was burnt down, Moscow could boast of no special importance, but it slowly began to acquire strength under its Prince Daniel, the youngest son of Alexander Nefsky.

Daniel's son George, who succeeded in 1303, continued his father's work, and added by force two towns to his domains, torn from those of neighbouring princes. Deterred by no scruples in his lust after power, he spent three years among the

Tartars, married the sister of their Khan Uzbek, and so insinuated himself into the favour of that mighty potentate that he was able to return to Russia with a diploma entitling him to the dignity of Grand Prince[1]—a dignity enjoyed at the time by Michael, Prince of Tver.

Against that Prince of Tver, George of Moscow commenced war, being assisted by Tartar auxiliaries; but he was put to flight, and his Tartar wife captured. Soon afterwards she died, and Michael of Tver, who was accused of having poisoned her, was ordered to appear before Uzbek Khan. The scenes which ensued, as described by the chroniclers, will serve to convey an idea of the degrading and perilous position in which the Russian princes of that time were often placed.

When the summons reaches the Prince of Tver, his boyars beseech him not to place himself within the power of the Tartars, but he replies,—

[1] It will be remembered that the various Princes of Russia acknowledge the supremacy of a Chieftain or Grand Prince. The Grand Princeship originally devolved upon the senior member of the princely family—seniority being defined according to old Slavonic custom. After the Tartar invasion the title depended upon the favour of the Khan, and that favour was chiefly enjoyed by the Moscow Princes, who eventually secured the title to their family, and made it hereditary.

"If I do not go my inheritance will be laid waste, and many Christian lives destroyed : better were it that I should die than that many should perish." And so he sets out for the neighbourhood of the mouths of the Don, where the tents of the Golden Horde are pitched. Uzbek Khan orders Michael, when he arrives, to be tried for having fought against the Tartars, and for having poisoned the wife of George of Moscow, Uzbek's sister. And the judges decide against the prince. At this juncture Uzbek Khan starts on a hunting expedition, and the unfortunate prince, who has not yet been sentenced, is dragged ignominiously after him. Southwards for twenty-five days he goes, a heavy piece of wood, probably like the *cangue* which Chinese criminals wear, attached to his neck, his hands fast bound together at night. But in spite of his bonds, after each day's journey is over, he spends the evening in reciting psalms, the psalter being held in front of him by a boy who turns over the pages for him as he reads.

At length the news comes that he is condemned to death. He assists at divine service, and afterwards takes leave of the clergy who attend on him, begging them to remember him in their prayers. Then he calls his young son to him, and confides to him his last wishes. And having done so, he asks for a psalter, opens it, and begins to read aloud the words, " My heart is disquieted within me, and the fear of death is fallen upon me." But the priests select another passage from the same psalm : " O cast thy burden upon the Lord, and He shall nourish thee : and shall not suffer the righteous to fall for ever." To which the prince replies with the verse, " O that I had wings like a dove : for then would I flee away, and be at rest."

Thereupon he closes the psalter. At that moment come tidings that Prince George of Moscow and a Tartar chief are approaching, followed by a great crowd. " I know wherefore they come," says Michael, with a sigh. Scarcely has he had time to send away his young son, when his murderers rush in. A few minutes later his naked corpse is flung outside his tent. Presently George of Moscow comes that way with the Tartar chieftain who had brought about Michael's death. And the Tartar shudders, and says to George, " Dost thou leave his body here to dishonour : was he not thy elder brother, even as it were thy father?" Then George orders it to be covered decently, and sends it to Russia, to be buried at Tver.

Next year George himself is summoned to the Horde to be tried by Uzbek. There Dimitry, son of the unfortunate Michael sees him, and, unable to bear the sight of his father's murderer, draws his sword, and slays him in the Khan's presence. So perishes George, Prince of Moscow, and his youngest brother Ivan rules in his stead.

In this Ivan I., surnamed Kalità,[2] Russian historians recognize the first consolidator of their country. Steadily keeping in view one end and aim, that of gaining power at the expense of his kinsmen, the other Russian princes, and by no means scrupulous as to the means by which that end was to be attained, he first secured the dignity of Grand Prince, then gradually extended the bounds of his own territory, and acquired the right of exercising a kind of control over at least some of the neighbouring principalities. Like his brother George, he ingratiated himself with the conquerors of his country; like his brother he did not hesitate to strengthen his position by bringing about the murder of a kinsman by Tartar hands. As George of Moscow had induced Uzbek Khan to slay

---

[2] The word *Kalità* means a purse or money-bag, and tradition says that Ivan (or Joann, our John) was called Kalità because he carried a purse from which he generously bestowed alms upon the poor. Bestuje Riumin thinks he may have thus been designated because he coined money.

Michael of Tver, so did Ivan persuade that Khan
to slay Michael's brother, the Grand Prince Alexander of Tver. His hatred of that unfortunate
kinsman is sufficiently intelligible, although the
mutual relations of the two princes are somewhat
complicated. Alexander had been named Grand
Prince by Uzbek, in succession to his brother,
Demetrius of the Terrible Eyes—the prince who
had avenged the murder of his and Alexander's
father, Michael of Tver, by slaying, in Uzbek's
presence, his virtual murderer, George of Moscow.
As Ivan of Moscow coveted the Grand-Princeship
he hated Alexander; in whom moreover he saw,
and perhaps feared, the son of the man whom his
brother George had done to death by evil words,
and the brother of the man to whose just wrath his
brother George had fallen a victim. Ivan's interests,
his hatreds, and perhaps his fears, all combined to
urge him to remove Alexander of Tver out of his
way; and before long chance gave him an opportunity of doing so.

It happened that in 1327, a Tartar Baskak, or
tribute collector, arrived in Tver with a large escort,
and began levying taxes in the rough and extor-
tionate manner for which the Baskaks were noto-
rious. In addition to the disquiet naturally produced
by such a visitor, a panic came upon the citizens of

Tver, caused by a rumour that he was about to compel them to discard their own religion and accept his. For this rumour there was not the slightest foundation. Neither when the Tartars first appeared as uncultured pagans, more or less imbued with Buddhistic doctrines, nor after they had accepted Mohammedanism, of which Uzbek was a fervent disciple, did they evince any desire to interfere with the religion of their Christian vassals. They even showed favour to the Russian clergy (whom alone of Russian men they exempted from the necessity of paying taxes); they allowed Christian priests to build a church, and to celebrate the rites of their faith, at the capital of the Golden Horde, Sarai ; and they made no sign of either indignation or uneasiness when their princesses married Russian princes, and accepted the religion of their husbands. Therefore the men of Tver might well have refused to listen to the ominous tidings : but, unfortunately for themselves, they lent ear to them, and coming together in hot haste they gave way to a wild fury, attacked the Tartars, overcame them towards the end of a day's hard fighting, and at last burnt all who survived of them in the palace in which they had vainly sought for shelter.

Uzbek not unnaturally swore to be revenged; but he left his vengeance to be wreaked by Russian hands. In obedience to orders received from the Golden Horde, Ivan of Moscow set out, at the head of an army, chiefly composed of Tartars, to punish his fellow-countrymen. At his approach, the Princes of Tver fled—the Grand Prince Alexander to Pskof, and his brothers to Ladoga. In a short time the Prince of Moscow was able to send tidings to the Horde that the capital of the Principality of Tver had been taken and sacked, that most of its towns were in ruins and its villages destroyed by fire, and that a great part of its inhabitants were dead or in captivity. The Tartar Khan received the news with joy, and, in return for such good service, conferred on Ivan the dignity of Grand Prince, of which Alexander of Tver was deprived. Alexander had fled to Pskof, the inhabitants of which independent city swore that they would not give him up. But the Prince of Moscow induced the Russian Metropolitan to lay Pskof under an interdict, whereupon Alexander said to them, "Friends and brothers! no curse shall fall upon you for my sake. I release you from your oath, and now I will go into Lithuania." Thither he went, and there he remained some time. Then he returned to Pskof, and spent ten years there. At the end of that time he made his peace with Uzbek Khan, and was restored to his Principality of Tver. Here again does the old chronicler give us a sad picture of these gloomy times.

When the Grand Prince of Moscow hears that Alexander has been restored to his princedom, he resolves on Alexander's ruin. So he also goes to the Horde, scatters money profusely there among the Khan's friends and advisers, and succeeds in blackening Alexander's character in the eyes of the Khan himself. Alexander is summoned to the Horde, and thither he repairs with a heavy heart, preceded by his young son Feodor. When, after his long journey, he reaches the Tartar camp, his son comes forth to meet him with sad tidings of the Khan's wrath. "God's will be done!" is the only reply uttered by Alexander. For a whole month he is left in suspense as to his fate. At the end of that time the sons of the Prince of Moscow arrive at the Horde, and on their representations Uzbek orders the Prince of Tver to be put to death. When Alexander hears the news he retires to his tent. For him and his son, as persons at the point of death, the rites of the Church are celebrated ; and then, after taking a last farewell of their weeping followers, the father and son go forth to meet their fate. They are slain, and a little later their mangled remains are solemnly interred in the Cathedral of Tver, by the side of that other victim of the malice of their Moscow kinsmen, Alexander's father Michael [3].

It was not the Tartar chief who was the gainer by Alexander's death. The whole advantage accrued to the Grand Prince of Moscow. [Uzbek did not know, nor was he likely to surmise, that the secret of Russia's weakness lay in the divided state of the country, that the overthrow of each petty ruler led to the increased power of the Prince of Moscow] and that a time would come when the principality of Moscow, having annexed the neighbouring states, would be strong enough to set its Tartar lords at defiance. But such was destined to be the course of events. Under Ivan's strict and grasping rule Moscow grew stronger and stronger every year. From the Cathedral of Tver he carried away its great bell, the summoner of the citizens to the assembly, the type and symbol of their municipal power. Over many of the other cities and princes he contrived to get a hold. Even from Novgorod, so proud of its independence, he extorted money. Of money he knew the value well, and therefore he gathered together treasures, and when need came did not grudge to spend them. Always

[3] Their deaths took place A.D. 1339.

on good terms with the Tartars, he obtained the privilege of levying the taxes imposed by them upon the Russian provinces, and of the sums which were supposed to pass through his hands no inconsiderable portion doubtless remained behind.

In addition to the power derived by the Prince of Moscow from his wealth and his interest at the Horde, great strength accrued to him from the favour shown him by the Church. Naturally devout and prone to implicit faith, the Russian people, soon after their conversion from heathenism, became warmly attached to their new religion. But, as was remarked at the close of the last chapter, after the Tartar invasions—at a time of so much bitter suffering, when the hearts of men were well-nigh broken, and in nothing earthly could solace or hope be found—it was natural that the people should more than ever turn their thoughts and aspirations heavenwards, and should become fervently devoted to the Church by whose means they tremblingly expected to obtain heavenly aid. Of this devotion Ivan I., conscious of its value, carefully availed himself. The earliest Russian Metropolitans resided at Kief, but after a while their seat was transferred to Vladimir. In the time of Ivan I., the metropolitan throne was occupied by Peter, a prelate afterwards enrolled among the saints of the Russian

Church. During one of his visitations he came to Moscow, and a strong mutual attachment grew up between him and Ivan I., to whom he afterwards paid frequent visits. On one of these occasions, the story runs, he bade the Grand Prince build a church and consecrate it to the Blessed Virgin, and provide him with a peaceful home beside its walls. And he promised that if Ivan would do so, great blessings would in return descend upon him and his. Ivan obeyed, and erected a stone church in honour of 'the Assumption of the Virgin, and the Metropolitan came to reside in Moscow, and after his death he was buried within the church. And his successor, Theognost, was unwilling to desert the home and the tomb of his wonder-working predecessor; and so from that time forward the Metropolitans continued to reside in Moscow—to the great advantage of Ivan I., and of the Moscow princes his successors.

What was of more advantage to the people than even the presence of the Metropolitan, was the comparative immunity they enjoyed from foreign invasion. Their Prince being on friendly terms with the Horde, their homesteads were no longer liable to be burnt by Tartar foes, their children to be carried into distant captivity. Freed from frequent danger and perpetual alarm they were, able to cultivate their lands in peace and to gather in their harvests with security. Under these favourable circumstances the inhabitants of the Moscow principality began once more to thrive, and their numbers to swell ; for the occupants of the other principalities, seeing what safeguards against ruin were afforded by Ivan's rule to his subjects, frequently left their former homes in order to take shelter on his territory and under his protection. At the same time he was always increasing his domains, either by force or by purchase. For being by far the richest of all the Russian princes, he was able to secure any outlying district which the poverty of its princely possessor might bring into the market, just as his wealth enabled him to outbid all other Russian competitors for the favour of the chief of the Golden Horde.

The death of Ivan Kalità, which took place in 1340, at first produced no change in the policy of Moscow. His successors continued to court the favour of the Tartars, and to encroach upon the other princes—to whom Kalità's son and immediate successor Simeon behaved so haughtily as to gain the designation of *Gordy*, or the Proud. Simeon was carried off by the Black Death, which at this time made terrible ravages in Russia. He was succeeded by his brother Ivan II., whose kindly and yielding disposition might have unfitted him for the stormy post he held had there not been by his side the keen-eyed and strong-willed Metropolitan of Moscow, Alexis. As it was, the other princes began, in his time, to offer a successful resistance to the growing power of Moscow; but their efforts were not sufficiently united or continuous to produce any great or permanent effect.

Passing over a few years, we find Dimitry, the son of the second Ivan, ruling at Moscow, and enjoying the dignity of Grand Prince, obtained only after a long and severe struggle. With the princes of Souzdal, Riazan, and Tver, Dimitry had to fight with all his strength. The last-named of the three princes was backed by the power of Lithuania; for Olgerd, Prince of Lithuania, was the brother-in-law of the Prince of Tver. Three times the Lithuanian forces invaded Russia, extending their ravages right up to the walls of Moscow; but each time the steady resistance of Dimitry forced them to retire. At length these wars and intestine struggles were brought to an end, and Dimitry was able to give his whole attention to a danger which threatened Russia from the East.

After a period of terrible disorder, during which

thousands of Tartars were destroyed by Tartar hands, the Golden Horde was now under the rule of a Khan named Mamai. To him Dimitry paid tribute, but only on condition that the Tartars refrained from all acts of violence against Russian subjects. In 1374 a disturbance was caused at Nijny Novgorod by some ambassadors from Mamai, against whom the people rose in tumult, and put them all to death. War on a small scale, and carried on with varying success, ensued between the Russians and the Tartars; but at length a crushing defeat of his troops enraged Mamai to such an extent, that he swore to wreak a terrible vengeance, and prepared for such an invasion as Baty's had been. It seemed as if the young life of Russia was doomed to perish under a storm similar to that which had all but annihilated the old political existence of the land.

Fortunately for the country, the influence of St. Alexis, the Metropolitan of Moscow, had sufficed to mitigate the mutual jealousy of the Russian princes, and to bind them together in a confederacy against the common foe of their church and their fatherland. One prince only, Oleg of Riazan, brought dishonour on his name by siding with the Horde against the Russian people—with the Crescent against the Cross.

Mamai's invasion, which took place in 1380, forms one of the most striking and romantic episodes in the history of Russia—one which it is impossible for us to regard, even looking at it as we do across so great a space of time, without a thrill of sympathy and of triumph. Let us try to call up before our mental vision some faint image of the scene which then presented itself to the eyes of the men of Moscow.

It is towards the end of the summer that Dimitry hears of the advance of Mamai's forces, and sends out messengers to summon the Russian troops to march from all parts of the country on Kolomna. Before long his own immediate forces are concentrated in Moscow, fresh bands of armed citizens pouring daily into the city from every side, until at length their organization is completed, and full of ardent enthusiasm they are ready to march against the foe. Before giving the word to start, however, Dimitry pays a visit to that famous monastery of the Troitsa or Trinity, which plays so important a part in Russian history, and there receives the benediction of its Superior, the sainted Sergius, who promises him a complete victory, though purchased by terrible bloodshed. Dimitry **returns to Moscow** full of hope, enters the Church **of St. Michael the** Archangel, and there, kneeling beside the tombs of his ancestors, prays for the success of his troops—troops which at this very moment are passing through the gates of the Kremlin, their colours flying, their arms glancing in the steady light of a day which seems, in its calm serenity, an omen of victory; while at their head in solemn array marches a long line of prelates and priests, bearing on high many a holy cross and icon, to which the people ascribe miraculous power. At length the Grand Prince issues from the church, embraces his wife, mounts his steed, and rides away to Kolomna.

From Kolomna such an army as Russia has never yet seen, numbering, it is said, 150,000 men, moves southwards towards the Don, beyond which river, Mamai, at the head of a countless host, is said to be awaiting the arrival of his ally, the Lithuanian Prince Yagello.[4] On the sixth of September the Russian forces reach the Don, and a council of war is held on the question whether to cross the river or not. Dimitry is on the point of adopting the advice of his more cautious counsellors,

[4] The Grand-Princedom of Lithuania which, during the fourteenth century, stretched from the Baltic to the Black Sea, must not be confounded with the Lithuania of the present day. Kief was seized by Gedimin in 1320, and it seemed an easy matter for Yagello to start from that city, meet Mamai, and march with him upon Moscow.

and stopping the march of his troops, when a message arrives, brought in hot haste from the Troitsa monastery. "Do thou go on," writes the holy Sergius, "and God will aid thee, and the Holy Mother of God." Then Dimitry gives the word to advance, and on the evening of the seventh of September the Russian forces begin to cross the "silently flowing Don."

Night comes on, dark, but warm and still. By the aid of legendary light—transmitted to us, it is said, by a contemporary poet—we see the Grand Prince ride out with the Voevoda, or leader of the Moscow troops, to inspect the field of the impending battle. Before them stretches out in the gloom the great plain of Kulikōvo. After riding over it for a time they halt and try to catch the meaning of the sounds they hear in the distance. From the Tartar side comes a strange uproar, loud and discordant, mingled with the distant howl of wolves and the cries of birds of prey; while from the banks of a neighbouring stream arises the constant plashing of water fowl, foreboding a coming storm. But on the Russian side all is calm and still; only the quiet shimmer of summer lightning plays along the horizon. This the Voevoda claims as a good omen. Then, dismounting from his steed, he lays his ear to the ground, and listens intently. When he rises tears are streaming from his eyes, and for a while he holds his peace. At length he says:—

"As I listened I heard the earth sorely lamenting. On the Tartar side the sound was like unto that of a mother mourning above her dead children. On our side it was as though a widow were wailing in her anguish. Thou wilt overcome the Tartars, but very many among the faithful will perish by pagan hands."

"God's will be done," replies Dimitry, and weeps bitterly. Then they two ride silently back to the camp, while behind them follow the howling of the wolves, and the croaking of the ravens, and the shrill cries of the eagles.

From this poetical picture [5] let us turn to the historical scene. The early morn of Saturday, September 8, is dark and misty, a thick fog brooding over the face of the land. But by the time the armies are set in battle array, the fog has risen and the sun shines brightly on the opposing hosts. The fight begins soon after mid-day, and is hotly contested on both sides. At length the Tartars gain the upper hand, and begin to drive the Russian troops before them. But the Russian reserve, under Dimitry's cousin, Vladimir the Brave, which has been set in ambush in a forest on the western side,

[5] Taken from the *Povyest' o Mamaevom Poboishchye*.

suddenly bursts from its hiding-place and falls upon the rear of the Tartar host as it sweeps by in full expectation of a complete victory. All is immediately changed. The Tartars are thrown into confusion by this unlooked-for attack; the Moscow troops face about and renew the fight. The Tartars waver; they give way. The Russians press them still harder. At last the Tartars take to flight, and fall by thousands at the hands of their pursuing conquerors.

When the battle is over, says a (doubtful) legend, Grand Prince cannot be found. Search the is made, and at length he is discovered, scarcely breathing, in a forest, under the branches of a hewn-down tree. His armour is shattered, but he has received no dangerous wounds, and his consciousness gradually returns to him as his cousin, Vladimir the Brave, congratulates him upon his victory.

Nearly five hundred years have passed away since that victory was gained.[6] But still the name of Dimitry Donskoi, or of the Don, lives in the memory and in the songs of the Russian people. Still on "Dimitry's Saturday," the anniversary of the day on which that good fight was fought, are solemn prayers offered up by the Church in pious

[6] In Sept. 8, 1380. The accent falls upon the diphthong in Donskoi.

remembrance of the thousands of Russian men who on that day fell in defence of their fatherland.

But this great victory was for a time doomed to be fruitless. Before long its brilliance was eclipsed by a new and sweeping storm of Tartar invasion, and even the lesson it ought to have taught, that united Russia could defy the Horde, was entirely forgotten. Mamai wrought no more harm to the Russian land; but his rival and dethroner, Tokhtamish, succeeded in accomplishing that which Mamai had failed to achieve. In 1382 a Tartar army entered Russia and marched straight upon Moscow. Dimitry Donskoi, some say, would have met the foe in the field as he had done before; but the other princes, perhaps jealous of the rising power of his principality, refused to co-operate with him, and he was obliged to retire with his family to Kostroma, and leave his capital to its fate. The citizens of Moscow, under the command of a Lithuanian prince named Ostei, retired into the Kremlin, and vigorously defended themselves against the foe. At last, Tokhtamish, under the guise of friendship, induced Ostei and some of the chief citizens to come forth from the Kremlin to an interview. In a moment Ostei and his companions were slain, and the Tartars rushing through the open gates soon overpowered all resistance, put to the sword or led away captive most of the inhabitants, and despoiled the churches of their gathered treasures, including a priceless library of manuscripts. From the capital the Tartars spread themselves over the whole principality, everywhere leaving desolation behind them, until, finding that Dimitry and his cousin Vladimir were in the field at the head of a considerable force, they hastily retired. Dimitry came back to his capital and found it a heap of ruins. His first task was to bury the dead, and so terrible had been the slaughter that some chroniclers say that 24,000 bodies had to be disposed of. Resistance to Tartar demands seemed after this terrible blow to be out of the question, and Russia once more relapsed into the state of servility and suffering which she had occupied before the worldly wisdom of the princes of Moscow had gained for her grace in the eyes of her Tartar lords.

We may pass rapidly over the space of time dividing the reign of Dimitry Donskoi, who died in 1389, from that of Ivan III., who began to rule in 1462. Fortunately for Russia, her terrible Eastern foes engaged in internecine war, and the battles of giants in which Tamerlane twice crushed the might of Tokhtamish permanently weakened the power of the Golden Horde. Still from time to time the

Russian provinces were laid waste. Thus we see Tamerlane, in chase of his defeated rival, cross the Volga and enter the south-east provinces of Russia, at the head of an army reckoned to consist of 400,000 men, "sowing death in the fields of the Christians." Along the banks of the Don he rides, terrible, seemingly irresistible. But Russia stands on her defence; Dimitry's son Vassily in the van, awaiting the approach of the colossal foe who had already swept like the scourge of God over so great a portion of the world. We see all Moscow a prey to anguish, her streets desolate, her churches filled with weeping crowds who refuse to be comforted, until at last the Grand Prince sends to the city of Vladimir for the famous picture of the Virgin which once before, as legends tell, has worked wonders for Russia. From the old to the new capital the picture is borne in solemn procession, most sorrowfully given up by the inhabitants of Vladimir, received with transports of joy by those of Moscow, who go forth in their thousands to meet it afar off, and reverently escort it to the Church of the Assumption within the Kremlin. On that same day, we are told, Tamerlane stops his march on the capital; his terrible array wheels to the south, and disappears beyond the Russian frontier. In gratitude for this unhoped-for deliverance, the Russian

Church still reckons among her festivals the 26th of August, keeping it holy every year as the anniversary of the day marked by Tamerlane's halt, and the "Reception of the Vladimir Icon of the Blessed Virgin."

Soon afterwards we see war declared between the two most powerful enemies of Russia—the Lithuanians, who are now masters of what used to be the principality of Kief, and the Tartars under their Khan Timur Kutluk. On the banks of the Vorskla the Lithuanian army is cut to pieces, and the principality of Moscow gains a brief respite, a short breathing time to recover from its wounds. Its Grand Prince even thinks himself strong enough to desist from rendering tribute to the Tartars, pleading the poverty of his land as a reason for paying the taxes into his own coffers; when suddenly, in 1407, the renowned Tartar chief Edigei, invades Russia and besieges Moscow, from which its Prince, the feeble Vassily, flies to Kostromà. Edigei encamps for a whole month before the walls of Moscow. Then he is recalled by his master, the Great Khan, but not before he has obtained a ransom from the beleaguered city.

In 1425, in the midst of a terrible period marked by famine and pestilence, by fire and by flood, when men's hearts are failing them because of their trouble, and to their tear-dimmed eyes the end of the world seems close at hand, the inglorious rule of Vassily, the son of Dimitry Donskoi, comes to an end, and in his place appears his son, also a Vassily, a boy only ten years old, doomed to many sorrows ere he dies. In his time countless evils come upon Russia, and among them civil war, cruel and long continued. It is indeed a gloomy picture which now presents itself to our view. We see the young Vassily set out with fear and trembling for the Horde. Quitting his capital on a fine summer's day, and casting back many a longing and tearful look at the gilded domes of its many churches, we see him on his return from the Horde installed in state as Grand Prince at the Golden Gate of his own cathedral by a Tartar official. And then we see the land given up to all the horrors of a civil war, waged between Vassily and an uncle of his who claims his title of Grand Prince. As the war goes on the shadows gather thicker and thicker. We see Vassily capture one of his uncle's sons, and in cold blood put out both the eyes of his unfortunate kinsman—a crime destined to bear a terrible fruit. Time goes by, but still we see Russia a scene of tumult and war. At length, in an encounter with the Tartars of Kazan, Vassily is taken prisoner; and when he is set at liberty, he finds his capital a heap of smoking ruins, among which a terrible conflagration has left but a few roof-trees standing.

Much has Vassily suffered, but his greatest suffering is still to come. During the night of the 12th of February, while the Grand Prince is absent from home on a visit to the Troitsa monastery, the Kremlin is suddenly seized by Prince Dimitry Shemyaka, brother of the prince whom Vassily blinded. Next morning, as Vassily is attending divine service beside the tomb of St. Sergius, tidings of the plot are brought to him, but he is unwilling to believe them. Soon, however, armed men are seen riding fast towards the monastery. Vassily recognizes his danger, runs to the stables, calls in vain for a horse, and then seeks refuge in the church. His enemies arrive, and the Grand Prince, vainly offering to abdicate and enter a monastery, is carried away to Moscow. And there, early next morning, in the palace of Dimitry Shemyaka whose brother he had blinded, he is himself deprived of sight.

Then follows an evil time in which Shemyaka, who has seized the throne of his blinded cousin, rules so violently, so persistently outrages justice, that his wrong doing passes into a saying, current to this very day among the Russian peasantry, who are wont to describe any unjust judgment as a *Shemyakin Sud*, a decision after the manner of Shemyaka. At length Vassily recovers his dominions, which he rules with a sagacity of which, until he became blind, he had showed no signs; and before he dies in 1462, he has the satisfaction of poisoning Dimitry Shemyaka, of striking a severe blow against the liberties of Novgorod and Pskof, and of strengthening his own power by crushing that of many of the princes his kinsmen.

To the wily but feeble Vassily the Blind succeeds, in 1462, one of the firmest and wisest sovereigns of whom Russia can boast—Ivan the Third, the Consolidater of the Russian Monarchy. On assuming the reins of power he finds himself at the head of a strong and all but united nation, the nominal lords of which, the once irresistible Tartars or Mongols, are disunited, and by no means in possession of their pristine strength. With one of the three branches into which their mighty host has split, the Tartars of the Crimea, Ivan III. concludes an alliance which before long becomes cemented into a friendship. With another branch, the Tartars of Kazan, he wages a war, which ends in their being for a time deprived of all power to inflict any serious wound on his realm. The third and strongest branch remains, that known as the Golden Horde. From his capital on the Volga, Sarai, the stately city founded by Batu, Ahmed Khan still issues his orders as Lord of the Russian land, still claims tribute from the Russian people and allegiance from the Grand Prince of Moscow. But the period of Tartar domination is fast drawing to an end. After Ivan III. has broken the proud spirit of the few cities which in Russia dispute his claim to permanent authority, and has rendered himself secure from being attacked by the Kazan or Crimean Tartars, he deems the time has come for dealing with the chief of the Golden Horde, and openly breaking the long since enfeebled bonds by which Russia has for more than two centuries been bound. In the days of Russia's degradation, when ambassadors from the Horde approached Moscow, it was the custom for the reigning prince to go forth on foot to meet them, to throw himself on the ground when they arrived, humbly kneeling to listen to the orders sent him by his supreme lord the Khan, and then respectfully to attend the ambassadors to their abode within the Kremlin. But urged by his proud consort, Sophia, the niece of the last Palæologus who reigned at Constantinople, Ivan III. refuses any longer to comply with the degrading customs by which the arrival of Tartar ambassadors has so long been accompanied; he even turns the ambassadors themselves out of their dwelling inside the Kremlin, on the pretext that his consort has been ordered in a vision to build a church upon its site. With such measures at least do legends credit the prince and his consort; going on to relate how, one day, when Tartar ambassadors appear before him, and call upon him to pay due reverence to the decree they bring from their master, Ahmed Khan—instead of bowing low as. have done his forefathers and predecessors, Ivan blazes forth with sudden and consuming fury, tramples the Khan's writing under foot, and puts to death all the ambassadors but one, whom he sends back to bid defiance to the ruler of the Golden Horde. The scene is an attractive one, and has given employment to the pencils of many artists. But it does not seem ever to have presented itself to any eye except that of fancy. Ivan III. was an exceedingly prudent statesman, and his actions were seldom due to mere impulse or a love of dramatic effect. But in the summer of 1480 we see by the steady light of history the forces of Ahmed Khan setting forth to invade Russia.

Along the confines of Russia do the Tartars ride, closely watched by the Russian forces. At length the two armies pitch their tents close together, divided only by the river Ugra. There Ahmed awaits the coming of his confederates the Lithuanians: but they do not come, for against them Ivan has detached his ally, the Khan of the Crimea. Unwilling to risk on a single chance all that Russia has gained during long years of prudent delay, the Grand Prince waits and strikes no blow. Presently he leaves the camp, and appears unexpectedly before Moscow. He finds the city full of alarm and trouble, the inhabitants of the suburbs flocking in to the Kremlin with their endangered treasures. Imagining that all is over, the Russian army annihilated, and the Grand Prince a fugitive from the battle-field, the people shower reproaches upon him. He rides to the Kremlin, but there also the Archbishop of Rostof addresses him with stinging words and hot reproaches. He sends for his son, but his son refuses to leave the army; he orders Prince Kholmsky to bring his son by force, but Prince Kholmsky disobeys. At length the Grand Prince yields to the desire of the nation, and leaves Moscow for the neighbourhood of the opposing camps. All the summer long Ahmed has remained quietly on the other side of the Ugra—"the Girdle of the Virgin," as the Russians call the river—

waiting till the frosts have made a bridge for him to cross. At last the winter sets in; the Ugra freezes. Then Ivan, on October 28, orders his troops to retire from the river to the spot where he holds his headquarters, and thence again to the neighbourhood of the town of Borofsk, probably intending to fight under its walls. But the retrograde movement of the Russian troops soon becomes first a confused retreat, and then a headlong flight, each man striving to save himself from the terrible Tartar horsemen whom he in fancy hears galloping behind. But no Tartars are galloping there. Instead of charging the broken and fleeing ranks, Ahmed tarries idly on the Ugra till November 11, and then retires to Sarai, wasting as he goes the territories of his defaulting Lithuanian ally. The Grand Prince returns in triumph to Moscow, where, in memory of a campaign so bloodlessly triumphant, the Metropolitan institutes an annual festival in honour of the Virgin, ordering that on a certain day of every year a solemn procession shall render thanks to heaven, and keep alive the memory of the day whereon Russia was at last freed from that Tartar yoke under which she had groaned so long.

For from the day when Ahmed commenced his

retreat, the Tartar subjugation was virtually at an end. Soon afterwards Ahmed was killed, and the power of his followers broken, by a rival Khan, who was content to receive presents from Moscow instead of demanding tribute. Before long the very name of the Golden Horde became for Russia no more than a memory of the past, and Sarai—Batu's splendid capital, the city towards which so many generations of Russian princes had journeyed in fear and trembling, within which so many of their number had sojourned in sorrow and humiliation, eating the bitter bread of dependence, and draining the cup of ignominy to its lees—Sarai, the home of the terrible chieftains who had pillaged and burnt so many Christian cities, who had crushed under the hoofs of their horses the liberties of Russia, and had set their feet upon the necks of her princes—this great city in its turn was stormed and sacked and burnt. And so complete was its ruin that gradually over its shattered walls, and its levelled palaces, and the mounds of refuse which marked where once had stood the houses of its citizens, there swept in its silent flow the soil of the steppe, until at last the site of the conquering capital could no longer be distinguished from the rest of the far-stretching plain, and its memory had entirely

I

died away from the minds of the neighbouring inhabitants.

Centuries rolled by, and at length, in the year 1840, an engineer who was mapping the Steppe, was struck by the regularity of undulation by which one part of the all but level plain was marked. So singular did it appear that he commenced excavating, and before long, at the depth of about a yard, he struck upon a granite wall. Excavations on a larger scale were immediately undertaken, and they resulted in laying bare the long-buried city of Sarai, with its innumerable streets, its royal palaces, its Russian quarter, in the midst of which the ruins of a Christian church were still recognizable, and its aqueduct, which, stretching over a distance of more than two miles, was wont to conduct to the Khan's palace, and to every part of the city, the once sweet waters of a lake long since grown salt.

As had been the fortunes of Sarai, so also had been those of the once conquering race whose chieftains had in bygone days ruled and revelled within its palaces. Long had that city been the advanced post of the terrible Eastern power which for two centuries and a half held Russia within its grasp and, during the earlier portion of that time, menaced all Western Europe with destruction.

It fell, and, before many years had passed away, the place thereof knew it no more. And as steadily as the soil of the steppe drifted over it, so did the power which it so long overawed wax stronger and stronger, until at length the whilom slaves of the East set their faces eastwards, and entered upon a course of Oriental conquest, the latest results of which have been the planting of their victorious banners upon the ramparts of Samarcand and of Khiva.

[A description of the ruin of Sarai will be found in Gerebtsof's " Civilisation en Russie," i. 222. Full accounts of the excavations are given in the Russian "Journal of the Ministry of the Interior" for 1845, 1847, etc. Sarai was the dwelling-place of " Cambuscan Bold," the hero of Chaucer's Squire's half-told tale beginning—
  " At Sarray in the land of Tartarye,
   There dwelt a kyng that werreyed Russye."
See Yule's " Marco Polo," i. 5, 6.]

CHAPTER V.

TSARDOM.

WE have now traced the history of Russia through three successive periods. Beginning with the arrival of Rurik, in a land of which only a small portion was peopled by Slavonians, we first watched the gradual rise, under princes of Scandinavian extraction, of the Slavonic state which, in the days of St. Vladimir, Yaroslaf I., and Vladimir Monomachus, became so widely renowned as the Grand Principality of Kief. Then we witnessed the confusion into which that state was changed after it became divided into a congeries of mutually repellent princedoms, united by few common interests, seldom obedient to any supreme law. And afterwards we caught a few glimpses of the period of tribulation through which the country was doomed to pass before the faults of its political constitution could be amended, and the possibility be offered to it of commencing a fresh career, of entering upon a new phase of existence. During the early part of that long period we saw the young civilization of Russia go down before the irresistible rush of Tartar barbarism, we heard the voice of lamentation rising from a land whose princes were so often steeped in ignominy, whose people were a prey to such constant fears of hurtful change; during the latter part of it we witnessed the gradual knitting together of the country around one salient point, the slow but steady increase of its vital power, the healthy development of its moral and physical resources, until the day came when it was able to measure its strength against that of its Oriental subjugators, and to fling off for ever the fetters which they had so long kept fastened upon its limbs.

In order to be able to present something like a continuous picture of the events to which Russia's relations with Asia gave rise, I have done no more than allude from time to time to the dangers which often threatened the safety of the land from the west. Still the name of Lithuania has been mentioned sufficiently often to demand, before we proceed farther, some explanation of its political importance. Beyond the western borders of

Russia there had dwelt from immemorial times the people called Lithuanians. Poor and uncultured, though possessing a copiously inflected language which they were altogether unaware was closely akin to Sanskrit, and inhabiting a land of swamps and forests, they long remained at a low level of both force and enlightenment, paying tribute (it is said) to the early Russian Princes, and at a later period undoubtedly suffering terrible ills at the hands of their German neighbours, the Knights of the Teutonic and Livonian Orders. At length there arose among them a prince named Mindovg, who belonged to the class of men from which spring the founders of barbaric monarchies, a chieftain strong-willed, intelligent, fearless, unscrupulous. Threatened with a simultaneous attack by the Russians and the German knights, Mindovg propitiated the latter by submitting himself to the Pope, and accepting at his hands (in 1252) the Christian religion and a royal crown.

Before he died, however, he killed the Master of the Livonian order, and solemnly abjured Christianity. Rather more than half a century after his death, in the year 1315, his throne became occupied by the real founder of the Lithuanian power. This prince, Gedimin by name, taking advantage of the weak state to which the Tartars had reduced

Russia, got into his power almost the whole of what, previous to the Tartar subjugation, had been Western Russia. His son Olgerd, as well as many of the Lithuanian nobles, accepted Christianity at the hands of Russo-Greek ecclesiastics: and so many of his subjects had previously been Christians, or subsequently became such, that in his time his capital Vilna is said to have possessed no less than thirty Christian churches. So much at that period did the state of his land assimilate itself to that of Russia, that the two countries might have become incorporated into one commonwealth, had not Eastern Russia been under the Tartar yoke.

During the reign of Yagello, Olgerd's son, the Polish crown passed to the young and beautiful Queen Jadwiga. For her hand, and for a share in that crown, Yagello became a suitor, offering to unite Lithuania with Poland, to pass from the Greek to the Latin Church, and to cause all his heathen subjects to be baptized. His plan was likely to be equally profitable to Lithuania and to Poland, neither of those countries being able single-handed to oppose its German neighbours. The Polish nobles accepted his offer, but Queen Jadwiga refused to do the same. She had been brought up from childhood in habits of intimacy with the Austrian Duke Wilhelm, and on him her young affections were set. Besides, she said, she was not going to marry a schismatic who was more like a wild beast than a man, and all covered over with shaggy hair. At last, however, she consented to accept him as her lord—when at that very moment, Wilhelm of Austria appeared at Cracow where she lived, obtained a private interview with her in a monastery, and induced her to marry him secretly. But immediately after the marriage rite had been celebrated, her Polish nobles seized the Duke and drove him away from Cracow. Jadwiga remained alone, a prey to the profoundest grief; until at last she learnt that Yagello was not the hirsute monster she took him for, but a handsome prince, of stately presence and of royal mien; whereupon she became consoled and married him. This took place in February, 1386. Towards the end of the year Yagello brought his royal bride to Vilna, and there gave orders that all his subjects should become Christians and members of the Church of Rome. The heathen Lithuanians were baptized in troops, the same Christian name being given to all the members of each band; the sacred groves were cut down, the holy fires were extinguished, and the snakes and lizards were destroyed which had so long been revered. In short, Yagello played at Vilna the same part which all but 400 years before

St. Vladimir had played at Kief. Many, however, of his subjects long remained heathens, and of those among his Christian subjects who belonged to the Greek Church, the greater part refused to alter their religious views. At length Yagello entrusted the rule of Lithuania to his brother Vitoft, who was succeeded at his death by another brother Svidrigello, and went southwards to carry on his government in Poland.

Such is the history of the foundation of the formidable Lithuanian-Polish monarchy, which was ruled over by Yagello (otherwise called Ladislas) and his descendants from 1386 to 1572. Had Lithuania and Poland, together with the western provinces torn from enfeebled Russia, been compactly welded together, had they been fused into one strong body actuated by one steady intelligence, its power might have proved too great for Russia to resist. But constant dissensions and even wars between the Grand Duchy and the Kingdom (which were not really united till 1569, just before the Yagello dynasty became extinct) saved Russia from being destroyed by its western foes—much as those foes interfered with its growth, often as they endangered its existence. At a later period, it is true, during the troublous times which preceded the accession of the first of the Romanofs, the

Poles actually succeeded in overrunning a great part of Russia, and Moscow was forced to acknowledge for a time a Polish Tsar, but their success was in a great measure the result of a series of accidents; or, to speak more correctly, of a series of crimes committed by Russian hands. The reign of Ivan the Third, with which we have now to deal, was darkened by no such misfortunes. Successful in almost all that he undertook, he regained in the north and north-west much that the Lithuanians had made their own; and when his realm was attacked and endangered by the Tartars of the Golden Horde, with whom the Lithuanians were in league, he completely foiled his western foes by opposing to them his trusty allies the Tartars of the Crimea. By skilful policy, by cautious diplomacy, rather than by force of arms, Ivan III. contrived to repress the enemies with whom he had to deal, on his western as well as upon his eastern frontiers. And he was no less successful in his great work of consolidating his power at home.

From the inhabitants of his own principality of Moscow, Ivan never had to fear opposition. They were entirely devoted to his person and submissive to his will. But at the period of his accession to power there still remained in Russia two classes of men whose views were to some extent antagonistic to those which he entertained. The first of these classes consisted of the other surviving princes of the house of Rurik, together with their supporters; the second comprised the inhabitants, of the various municipalities. To these two divisions of the body politic it may be as well to turn our attention for a while.

To begin with the Princes. We have already seen to what evils the system of appanages gave rise. Time after time the Russian land, after thriving prosperously under a single ruler—a Vladimir or a Yaroslaf, for instance—became plunged into countless troubles on his death, owing to the ceaseless feuds between the rival heirs among whom he divided his domains. The system under which so many princes became entitled to distinct and all but independent territories has been explained by different Russian historians in very different ways. We need not in this chapter enter into any discussion of their views. But it is important to bear in mind, says Bestujef-Riumin, that, in spite of all the divisions which took place, Russia maintained some kind of unity. The Russian princes never looked upon each other as utter strangers; the Russian community always considered itself an integral community. In the midst of men of hostile religions and of alien blood, the Russian people was kept together by the princely *drujinas*, or bands of military retainers, and by the kindly bonds of its Christian faith.

At first, as we have seen, the principality of Kief stood pre-eminent, and it long maintained its high position. But at length its power began to decline, and after being sacked, first by Russian and then by Tartar hands, it at last passed into the power of the Lithuanian princes. Next in order was the principality of Souzdal: the land of that division of the Russian people which is known as the Velikorussky or Great Russian.

Colonies from Novgorod and White Russia are supposed to have gone thither, and as they were constantly clashing with the Finnish inhabitants of the basin of the Volga, they were obliged to lead a vigorous and watchful life. For a long time the Grand-Princeship remained associated with the city of Vladimir, as it had formerly been with the city of Kief. Then Moscow arose: and after a time the Moscow princes, owing to their influence at the Golden Horde, succeeded in first obtaining the dignity of Grand Prince for themselves, and then in making it hereditary in their family. We have seen that partly by force, partly by intrigue, partly by purchase, Ivan I., called Kalità, the founder of the supremacy of Moscow, got into his own hands the territories of many of the other princes, his kinsmen. By his time cunning had become more important than force. The Grand-Princeship depended not upon strength, but upon skill in obtaining a diploma from the Khan of the Golden Horde; and in this skill the Moscow princes were unrivalled. "All these Moscow princes," says Solovief, "were alike one to another: in their passionless faces it is difficult for the historian to discern each one's characteristic traits. They are all imbued by one idea, they all walk in one path: and that slowly, cautiously, but uninterruptedly, inflexibly. Each one makes a step in advance of his predecessor; each one renders it possible for his successor to advance a step beyond him."

This cautious character is explained by their position. They were not naturally strong. They were not originally rich. Their province was a poor one, their city an unimportant town, their chief river a shallow stream, and that at a time when the rivers formed the principal highways of the land. It is true that Moscow occupied a central position, near the sources of the chief rivers, and on this advantage one Russian historian lays stress, but another thinks it of no great importance. The causes which really conduced to the steady development of the Moscow Principality, seem to have been :—

1. The cautious policy of its princes—who knew how to bow down low before the Golden Horde while it was strong, and to smite it hard when it grew weak.

2. The favour shown to the Princes of Moscow by the clergy—who saw how advantageous for them (says Miliutin) would be the concentration of all the scattered principalities under the power of a single Tsar, and therefore were always devoted to their views and their policy.

3. The assistance given to those princes by the Moscow boyars, who played an important part in the administration of public affairs, especially during such long minorities as those of Dimitry Donskoi and Vasily II. Having been accustomed to be the boyars of a Grand Prince (says Solovief), they did not like to play a secondary part. And therefore they did all they could to preserve the Grand-Princeship in the family of the chief whom they had served.

Such were the principal causes which enabled Moscow first to rival, and then to absorb, the other principalities. But they would have acted in vain had not the power of the Golden Horde broken down exactly at the right time. As it was, all things seemed to work together for the benefit of the principality of which, as we have already seen, Ivan I., surnamed Kalità, was the virtual founder; the first prince who assumed the title of "Great Prince of all Russia"—a title perhaps created, says Bestujef-Riumin, in imitation of that of the Metropolitan. His elder son, Simeon the Proud, continued his policy towards the rival princes; and if it was suspended for a time during the rule of Kalità's younger son Ivan II., who succeeded his brother Simeon the Proud, it was resumed by the son of Ivan II., the celebrated Dimitry Donskoi. That prince is generally remembered as the gainer of the battle of Kulikóvo, a battle which, Solovief thinks, was as important to the fortunes of Eastern Europe as were the battles of Chalons and of Tours to those of Western Europe. It served as the turning point of the Asiatic movement upon Europe. Soon after its time began the European movement upon Asia. But even when due importance has been attached to it, there still remains good reason for regarding Dimitry Donskoi in the light rather of an administrator than of a general. Terrible in his relations with the other princes, severe towards even his own boyars, Dimitry maintained the stern and aggressive policy commenced by his grandfather Ivan Kalità, and gave the state he ruled such an impetus as carried it safely through the periods marked by the inaction of his son Vassily I., and the misfortunes of his grandson Vassily II., the Blind.

Even under the sway of its feebler rulers, the patrimony of the Moscow princes was always increasing. One after another the appanaged princes, tricked, or bought, or crushed, gave up or were deprived of their rights; and when Ivan III., the great-grandson of Dimitry Donskoi, succeeded to the throne, he was already in a position which bade fair to become, so far as the other princes were concerned, that of a supreme ruler. ⟨Before his long reign came to an end, he was all but the supreme ruler of Russia; the princes whose ancestors, in former times, had rivalled or ruled his being content to figure as his officers of state.⟩

During the reign of his son, Vassily Ivanovich, the last remains of the appanage system disappeared, and the Grand Prince of Moscow was left without a single rival within his domains who could contest his right to rule as Autocrat of all Russia. ⟨About the time when the feudal system was yielding to the attacks of autocracy in Western Europe, the appanage system collapsed in what constituted a large portion of Eastern Europe.⟩

This successful struggle with the rival princes was carried on almost entirely without bloodshed. According to a courtly historian, the vanquished were overcome more by a sense of their own unworthiness and the enormous merits of the Prince of Moscow than by aught else; but other writers are rather inclined to attribute the result to the unscrupulous persistency with which the Moscow princes carried out their traditional policy, the steadiness of their yearning after new acquisitions, the tenacity of their grip when they had once succeeded in acquiring.

With the great municipalities it was not possible to deal in so bland a manner. Novgorod and Pskof, though nominally subject to princes, had really maintained for centuries a species of independence almost republican. In Novgorod the Vetché, or Common Council, had always been more powerful than elsewhere; with Novgorod it was usual for its princes to enter into real contracts, such as in other cities existed only under a more elementary form. The restrictions on the Novgorod prince were numerous. He was obliged to govern according to old custom. He might be judged, sentenced, and expelled by the Vetché, or General Assembly, and he was obliged to pay due deference to the great municipal officers, the Possadnik, the city's civil ruler, and the Tysiatsky, its military chief. All this independence was partly due to the geographical position of Novgorod — situated in a swampy and sterile district, but enjoying the advantages accruing to it as a great commercial centre, the link between the commerce of the East and of the West. To its situation, also, is probably owing its happy escape from Tartar invasion—an escape which confirmed and ensured its long-maintained independence. Somewhat similar reasons had conduced to the freedom of Pskof. A Novgorod colony, planted like an outpost on the confines of Russia, its domain a long slip bordering on the Lithuanian and German territories—that city was obliged by its position to be ever on its guard, and to keep up a warlike spirit among its citizens, while its proximity to powerful strangers enabled it to make easy terms with its own rulers.

But the independence of Novgorod and of Pskof was not consistent with the ideas entertained by Ivan III. Before he had been long in power he determined to make his authority supreme over the proud and turbulent burghers of those ancient municipalities.

It is difficult to see clearly through an atmosphere

heavily charged with intrigue, but if we turn our eyes towards Novgorod, we distinctly discern among the leading inhabitants of the city the figure of Marfa Boretskaya, the widow of the late Possadnik Boretsky, a bold and ambitious, possibly also a patriotic woman. Under her guidance the city determines to throw off its allegiance to Ivan III., and to transfer it to Casimir, King of Poland and Grand Duke of Lithuania. Accordingly a solemn compact is entered into with that monarch, under the impression that the Grand Prince of Moscow will be afraid or unable to do more than protest. But Ivan assembles his troops and wages war against the rebellious city—war swift and severe. Aided by the men of Pskof, his troops bear down all resistance. After a short time Novgorod the Great is obliged to surrender, and to accept Ivan as her ruler: he swearing, however, to govern the city according to its ancient statutes.

All this takes place in 1471. A few years pass by; fresh complications and new disputes arise. It becomes the custom for suitors, especially if they belong to the Moscow party, to appeal for justice to Ivan III. when they think they are wronged at Novgorod. Among the number of those who for this purpose visit Moscow in 1477 are two envoys from the city on the Volkhof, and they in their petition style Ivan their *Gosudar*, or Monarch. Now the men of Novgorod have never yet called Ivan their Gosudar, but only their Gospodin, or Master. Ivan sends to Novgorod to ask what sort of *Gosudarstvo*, or monarchy, the citizens desire of him. When the General Assembly hears this a great uproar arises, and the people shout, " It is a lie ! Never was there a time when we called the Prince our Gosudar." And they lay hands upon some of the Moscow partizans and put them to death.

Tidings reach Ivan that Novgorod is about once more to submit itself to the Polish king, and he prepares again for war. A little later we see the Novgorod territory overrun and wasted, and the city itself invested on every side. Its supplies soon run short, and the people begin to perish by famine and disease. The mob rises against the nobles; the nobles strive to crush the power of the mob. Novgorod is in its death agony ; its last hour of independent existence is at hand.

On January 15, 1478, the city submits to Ivan's terms. They are—that in future he shall govern it despotically, as he governs his own Moscow ; and that its citizens shall no · longer enjoy the right of assembling in the Vetché, or possess the great bell which used to summon them to that assembly. So their bell is taken down and sent to Moscow: whither the great bell of Tver has gone before it.

No longer do the Novgorod people hear it "swinging slow with solemn roar," and wakening in their hearts fond memories of ancient independence maintained on many a hard-fought field. But still they find it difficult to forget old days, and again they make an attempt to struggle against the power of Moscow. And again they are crushed by Ivan, who this time puts many of the conspirators to death, and sends away thousands of the Novgorod people into other provinces, replacing them by Muscovites, or inhabitants of the principality of Moscow.

At this point the history of independent Novgorod virtually comes to an end. Pskof is allowed to survive its fellow republic for a time; but if we look forward to the reign of Ivan's successor, we shall see its liberties also crushed beneath the wheels of the relentless car of autocracy. It is easy for the Tsar to find a cause of complaint against its citizens; it is impossible for them to plead their cause successfully against his interests.

Meeting together in their General Assembly, they listen to the hard terms offered to them by the Tsar Vassily III.—listen all but in silence, and then ask for a day's grace in order that they may consider them. Terrible are that day and night for the people of Pskof—" only the infants at the breast are exempt from the general distress," says their annalist. The next day the bell summons the citizens for the last time to their council. They meet and deliberate sadly, but not without dignity. At length they yield, and take down from its belfry the type and symbol of their ancient and dearly-loved liberties, the great bell which is now doomed to follow to Moscow the bells of Novgorod and of Tver. Thus mournfully ends for them the 13th of January, 1510, the day on which perishes the last remnant of the old municipal liberties of Russia.

Returning now to the reign of Ivan III., we find him, by the year 1480, free from all danger of being effectually opposed, or even temporarily annoyed, either by the members of the princely family or by the great municipalities. And therefore he is able to turn his whole attention towards the Asiatic foes who have so long domineered over Russia, and who [are just now threatening once more to lay waste its fields.

What came of those threats we have already seen.[1] We watched the cloud gathering in the south-

[1] See above, pp. 110—112.

east. We traced its progress across the Don and right up into the centre of Russia, till it hung, and for a protracted period of suspense remained hanging, ominous, motionless, along the line of the river Ugra. And then we saw it retire, devastating as it went the fields of the Lithuanians, till at last it disappeared amid the Steppes of the Caspian, and Russia could once more breathe freely beneath the open sky.

CHAPTER VI.

TROUBLOUS TIME.

AT the end of the fifteenth century we reach a point at which the "early history" of Russia may fairly be brought to a close. Towards the end of the life of Ivan III., the Russian land appears to have the prospect before it of entering upon a new and prosperous phase of existence. From being an inert congeries of feeble and discordant states it has become a vigorous commonwealth, to a great extent subservient to general interests, almost entirely obedient to one strong will. Wave after wave of foreign invasion has swept over it, and at times it has seemed to be on the point of being absorbed in the sweeping flood of Eastern barbarism, but now the tide appears to be about to set in an opposite direction. Russia's turn for foreign conquest seems to have arrived.

Here, then, we might well pause. But before actually turning our eyes aside from the fortunes of the country, let us cast a rapid glance over the events by which the century following the death of Ivan III. is chiefly rendered remarkable.

The reign of Vassily Ivanovich, so far as its internal policy is concerned, may be looked upon as a prolongation of that of his father, Ivan III. There is no break in the continuity of Muscovite progress; the machinery of state works unaltered, though the guiding hand of the chief engineer has been changed; the stream of national life flows on in the same narrow, but deepening channel, into which its long-scattered waters have been of late directed. Vassily is inferior in intellect to his father, but he is his equal in acquisitiveness and tenacity. Even more despotic than Ivan III., he will not tolerate the slightest opposition to his will. Nor do many of his subjects think of opposing it. There are but few among Russian men who do not style themselves his slaves, who refuse to acknowledge in him God's vicegerent, who are not wont to use the conventional expression employed about any doubtful matter: " God and the Gosudar will see to that."

In his dealings with the greatest of Russia's western foes, Lithuania, Vassily's policy is generally successful. He fails, indeed, in his attempt to induce the Polish and Lithuanian nobles to elect him their king, on the death of his brother-in-law Alexander, in 1505. But in 1514 he succeeds in wresting from Alexander's successor, Sigismund, the important city of Smolensk, which has for a hundred and ten years been held by its Lithuanian conquerors. During the same year, it is true, a terrible loss is nflicted on the Russian forces by the Lithuanians at Orsha, on the left bank of the Dnieper, where 30,000 of Vassily's troops are said to have fallen. But this apparently crushing victory produces no lasting results. In 1517 Vassily destroys all that remains of independence in Riazan, a territory which during four hundred years has formed a distinct principality, one of the few "appanages" to which Ivan III. conceded some shadow of separate authority. A little later falls another princedom, that styled Séverskoe. Its last ruler is imprisoned at Moscow in 1523, and tradition tells how a *Yurodivy*, a sort of Christian fakir or dervish, goes wandering about the city at that time ; holding a broom in his hands, and replying to all questions as to his meaning, " The realm is not yet quite purged ; and the time has come for sweeping out the last of the rubbish:" thereby signifying that an end ought to be made of the last remains of the appanage, or independent-princely system.

With Russia's Oriental foes Vassily does not fare so well. The power of the Golden Horde is extinct, but the two other branches of the great eastern host which settled in the neighbourhood of Russia after the wave of Mongol conquest had burst upon Europe in the thirteenth century, the Tartars of the Crimea and of Kazan, are sufficiently strong to keep the Muscovite princes in constant disquiet. And so in 1521 we see one Tartar force advance from the south, completely rout the Russian army on the banks of the Oka, and unite at Kalomna with another Tartar force which has marched thither from Kazan. Onwards go the still terrible descendants of the irresistible barbarians who so often swept over Russia in previous centuries. Burning the villages and laying waste the fields as they go, they reach the Sparrow Hills, and from their brow look down upon the capital of the Tsar. Within the walls of Moscow all is fear and confusion. The Tsar has fled, the inhabitants of the burning villages in the neighbourhood are flocking into the Kremlin, carrying with them their old people and little children and what they could save of their property—doing, in fact, just what their forefathers had in old times so often been forced to do. But the siege of the capital is not pressed. Vassily agrees to pay tribute to the Crimean

Khan, who thereupon retires to Riazan. That city he attempts to seize by treachery, but a seasonable discharge of artillery, due to the prudence of " one Johann Jordan, a German, who came from the Innthal," foils his plans, and he hastily withdraws to the Crimea, leaving behind him the humiliating document by which the Orthodox Tsar has bound himself to pay tribute to the infidel. But with him go thousands of Russian captives—eight hundred thousand says tradition—destined to be sold or slain. "The old and infirm men, who will not fetch much at a sale, are given up to the Tartar youths (much as hares are given to whelps by way of their first lesson in hunting), either to be stoned, or to be thrown into the sea, or to be killed by any sort of death they may please [1]."

The year after this Tartar invasion we see Vassily disquieted by family troubles. After twenty years of married life he is still without offspring. One day, says an annalist, as he is driving in the neighbourhood of Moscow, he sees a nest in a tree. His eyes fill with tears as he laments over his childless lot, and on his return home, he resolves to put away his barren wife. Soon afterwards she is forced to take the veil, protesting, broken-hearted, in the presence of all that she does so " unwillingly

[1] Herberstein, " Notes upon Russia," ii. 65.

and under compulsion ; and invoking the vengeance of God on her behalf for so great an injury²."

A few years later we witness an unseemly squabble arising on the occasion of monastic attire being donned by her cruel lord. In the summer of 1533, Vassily, while absent from Moscow on a hunting expedition, is seized by a terrible illness. He is brought back with difficulty to his palace in the Kremlin, and there, after a last interview with his second wife and his children by her, he asks for the monastic tonsure and habit. The clergy who are present hasten to comply with his request, but some of the boyars protest, and even strive to snatch the black robe from the hands of the Metropolitan. But the priests prevail ; Vassily is invested with the monkish insignia. A few moments later his death is announced to the crowd which waits anxiously outside, and the members of the royal family and the great nobles are called upon to swear allegiance to Vassily's young son, Ivan, and to his mother Helena Glinsky.

Over the reign of that son, Ivan IV., justly styled the Terrible, it is well to pass rapidly. English eye-witnesses[3] have narrated for us the

> ² Herberstein, " Notes npon Russia," ii. 51.
> ³ Dr. Jerome Horsey, and Dr. Giles Fletcher.

tragedies which threw so black a shadow over the second portion of that savage despot's career. To their pages may be referred all admirers of such " strong government " as despotism pure and simple can offer. Sufficient for our purposes will be the hastiest glance. By it is first revealed to our eyes the long minority of the boy-tsar. We see him left to the mercy of the ruling boyars, who develope all that is bad in his nature, deliberately corrupting him in order to keep him, and with him the royal power, under their own control. We see him on the one hand trained to act cruelly, encouraged to torture and kill animals, and on the other hand treated with such insolence and even outrage as were certain to bear evil fruit at a later time. And so, when he is old enough to take into his own hands the management of affairs, we see him yielding to cruel revenge, as well as to malicious pleasantry and degrading licentiousness.

Then comes the second period of his life in which, alarmed by the terrible conflagrations which have reduced his capital to ruins, and by the popular outbreaks to which they give rise, the wild prince who has so long been surrounded by dissolute minions, suddenly changes into a dignified monarch, watchful as a statesman, courageous as a general, benevolent as a legislator. Then before our eyes is unrolled the long panorama of the siege and capture of Kazan—a prose epic in itself, full of picturesque scenes, of dramatic recitals. Thirteen years go by during which Ivan so behaves that, if he had died at the end of that time, his memory would have been hallowed by history as that of a wise and good monarch.

But then arrives the third period of his life, that in which he acts in full accordance with his designation of "The Terrible." After his illness and the death of his wife Anastasia, the evil side of his nature once more heaves slowly into sight. He destroys the true friends who have hitherto succeeded in guiding him aright, he attacks every noble who will not blindly obey his orders, and he develops a taste for blood which at last, aggravated by a constant suspicion of treachery, impels him on a course of cruelties such as the world has seldom known. Thus there is scarcely another page of history so bloodstained as that which tells how the innocent people of Novgorod were punished for a treason which had never existed except in the imagination of the wretches who, on the testimony of documents forged by themselves, falsely asserted that it had taken place.

It is in January, 1570, that Ivan arrives with his troops in Novgorod. We see him attend divine service n the cathedral, and then take his seat at the banquet which the Archbishop has prepared for him. Suddenly he utters a wild cry. In rush a crowd of armed men, the Archbishop is seized and cast into prison, and his palace is pillaged in the Tsar's behalf. A little later Ivan lets loose his wrath upon the trembling city. Its leading citizens are tortured and slain; numbers of them, together with their wives and children, being flung into the Volkhof, while the Tsar's retainers ride along the banks of the river in order to prevent any of their victims from escaping. For five whole weeks, it is said, does this terrible butchery go on. To this very day a tradition exists among the common people that, owing to the immense quantity of human blood then poured into the Volkhof, that river never freezes in the neighbourhood of the bridge, however severe the winter may be. And to this day may the burial-place of Ivan's victims be easily recognized near one of the churches of Novgorod, the slightest disturbance of the soil showing that the ground is full of human bones.

From Novgorod Ivan goes on to Pskof, where the panic-stricken citizens, awaiting a doom like that passed on Novgorod, fling themselves prone at his feet, and receive him with trembling offerings of bread and salt. It may be that their humility touches his savage heart, it may be that he is stung by the taunt attributed to the *Yurodivy* Nicholas, who offers him a piece of raw flesh. " I am a Christian and eat no flesh during a fast," cries the Tsar. " But thou doest worse," replies Nicholas, " thou dost eat the flesh of men." Moreover he threatens the Tsar with terrible evils in case the inhabitants of Pskof are injured, and Ivan, as superstitious as he is brutal, retires from the city with his thirst for blood unslaked.[4]

Of the horrors which mark the Tsar's return to Moscow we are not called upon to speak

" Non ragioniam di lor, ma guarda e passa."

In the spring of 1571 we see the Crimean Tartars marching upon Moscow, whence Ivan flies, leaving the city to its fate. A fire breaks out during a gale of wind, and in a few hours Moscow is reduced to ashes, thousands of its inhabitants, says Horsey, " being burnt and smothered to death by the fierce eyre," or drowned in the river, which " could not be ridd nor clensed of the dead carcasses in twelve

---

[4] "I saw this impostur or magicion," says Sir Jerome Horsey, (p. 162) speaking of the *Yurodivy* Nicholas—" a fowll creature, (who) went naked both in winter and sommer ; he indured both extreame frost and heat ; did many strcinge things thorow the magical illusions of the Divell," etc.

L.

monneths after." Nor is this the only loss suffered by Russia. From the Poles and Lithuanians and the Swedes also the land has to undergo insult and injury, and on its suffering inhabitants press heavily famine and pestilence. Meanwhile Ivan continues his cruelties, incessantly tormented by fear of treachery, haunted at times by the recollection of his sins. At one time we find him inquiring whether in case of need he can count on an asylum in England ; at another he is meditating a matrimonial alliance with our Queen Elizabeth. Finding that impossible, he sets his heart on marrying Lady Mary Hastings, daughter of the Earl of Huntingdon. Not without some touch of humour does Horsey describe the interview between that lady and the ambassador whom Ivan sends to arrange the marriage. "The ambassador, attended with divers other noblemen and others, was brought before her ladyship ; cast down his countenance ; fell prostrate to her feett, rise, ranne backe from her, his face still towards her, she and the rest admiringe at his manner. Said by an interpritor yt did suffice him to behold the angell he hoped should be his master's espouse ; commended her angelicall countenance, state and admirable bewty." More in keeping with the gloom hanging about Ivan's reign is a second picture drawn by Horsey, in which most sadly figures another person connected with the scheme for an English marriage, Dr. Eliseus Bomelius. He, after being racked, "his arms drawen backe disjointed, and his leggs streiched from his middle loynes, his backe and bodie cutt with wyer whipps," was taken from the rack, bound to a stake and "rosted and scorched till they thought noe liff in him." Then he was cast into a sledge and "brought thorrow the castell," where Horsey "preste among many others to see him." He "cast up his eyes naminge Christ," after which he was flung into a dungeon to die.

It is in November, 1581, that the mad Tsar attains the climax of his crimes in the murder of his eldest son; whom he smites on the head with so violent a blow from his iron staff that the prince falls insensible, and after a few days expires. Then despair seizes for a time upon the Tsar, who can rest neither by day nor by night, and who tries to expiate his crimes by gifts to monasteries and churches, and by having prayers said for the victims of his wrath; causing them to be prayed for by name when his memory serves him, and in other cases entreating God to have mercy upon the souls of such men as "Thou, O Lord, knowest." At last, in the beginning of 1584, he is smitten by mortal illness. Horsey's narrative gives a vivid picture of the last scene of his eventful history. We see the dying tyrant sending for magicians "out of the North, wher ther is store." They arrive, threescore in number, and being consulted by Prince Belsky, tell him that the "strongest planetts of heaven" are against the Tsar, and will produce his end by a certain day; whereupon Prince Belsky replies that they are "veri likly to be all burnt that daye." We see the dying monarch daily carried into his treasury, where one day he explains to his nobles, in Horsey's presence, the virtues of his various jewels. At length the day arrives which the magicians have said will be his last. Prince Belsky visits them, and taunts them with the failure of their prediction. "Sir, be not so wrathfull," they reply; mindful, perhaps, of the first Cæsar and the Ides of March; "you know the daie is com, and ends with the settinge of the sun." About midday the Tsar calls for a chess-board and sets his pieces in order, "all savinge the king, which by no means he could not make stand in his place with the rest upon the plain board." Suddenly he faints, falls backward, and all is over.

Ivan the Terrible leaves behind him two sons, Feodor and Dimitry. On the 4th of May, 1584, the *Duma*, or Council, proclaims Feodor Tsar, and for nearly fourteen years he nominally reigns—a true *roi fainéant*, under the guidance of a really reigning *maire du palais*, his wife's brother, Boris Godunof. Not as an imposing monarch does he figure in Dr. Giles Fletcher's unflattering narrative [5], but at the same time not as an unkindly one.

In appearance he is " of a meane stature," sallow, " hawke-nosed," unsteady in his gait, "heavie and unactive, yet commonly smiling almost to a laughter." In character he is "simple and slowe-witted, but verie gentle, and of an easie nature, quiet mercifull, of no martial disposition, nor greatly apt for matter of policie, very superstitious, and infinite that way."

Very different from this feeble but well-meaning monarch is his firm and unscrupulous brother-in-law. The story of his rapid rise is one of the strangest to be found even in Russian history. During the fourteenth century, a Tartar Mirza or Noble, named Chet, becomes a convert to Christianity, and is baptized under the name of Zachary. His grandson, Ivan Godun, is the founder of the Godunof family, which thrives and grows powerful. At length the Tsarevich Feodor marries Irina Godunof, and after his accession to the throne, her

[5] *Russe Common Wealth*, p. 144. This is one of the passages on account of which the book was suppressed.

brother Boris becomes the actual ruler of the Russian Monarchy. Sharp-witted, keen-eyed, cautious and patient, he quietly bides his time. Utterly selfish and unscrupulous, he is ready to commit any crime in order to attain to the one end and aim of his life, the aggrandizement of his own family; but free from the senseless fears and hatreds of Ivan the Terrible, he is not disinclined to perform good and kindly actions, when they in no way impede his progress or endanger his interests.

So far as the Tsar Feodor is concerned, Boris acts with wisdom and fairness. From him he has nothing to fear. The Tsar is soft-witted, and likely to die young, and—after the death of an infant daughter—without leaving issue. Boris can afford to wait patiently for his death, and then to claim for himself the vacant throne. But two other members of the royal family stand in his way. Of them it is necessary that he should be rid. They are the Tsarevich Dimitry, Feodor's half-brother, younger son of Ivan IV., and Ivan's cousin [6] Maria, the widow of Magnus, Duke of Holstein and titular King of Livonia. Her, and her young

[6] She is generally called his niece, but she was really his "first cousin once removed," being the granddaughter of Ivan's uncle Andrew, a younger son of the tsar Ivan III.

daughter Eudoxia, he contrives by fair but false words to lure into Russia from her abode in Riga, using as his agent our countryman Jerome Horsey. For a while she is treated with all respect and courtesy, but after some time she is separated from her child and immured in a convent. In 1589 the young Eudoxia is buried in the Troitsa monastery. All honour is paid to her remains, as to those of a member of the royal family, but an impression prevails throughout the land that she has been put to death by Godunof's orders. Well may that highly respectable country gentleman, Sir Jerome Horsey, when writing his account of how he helped to lure the widowed mother and her fatherless child into the hands of the destroyer, conclude with these words : " This pece of service was verie acceptable : whereof I much repent me." Often let us hope that he, sitting in his happy English home, by the side of that "honest gentleman's daughter of Buckinghamshire," his wife—grand-aunt of John Hampden—thought with some compunction of the day when he first saw the widowed Queen " comynge of her daughter's head and hear, a proper gerrell of nien years of age :" when she placed her trust in him, saying with tears, " Sir, your countenance, speach and atier, makes me to believe you more than reason can persuade me," little thinking that he would some day have to write: that "she exclaimed 'Woo be unto the tyme she was betraied and that ever she gave faithe to me.'"[7]

Only the Tsarevich Dimitry now stands between Boris and his prospect of some day mounting the throne. The young prince is residing with his mother and several of her kinsmen in a kind of honourable exile at Uglitch, on the Volga. As some of Godunof's retainers have lately arrived in the town, the boy is jealously guarded by his relatives. But one day—it is the 15th of May, 1591—about noon, when most of his guardians have gone away to dinner, the tocsin is heard sounding from the bell-tower of the cathedral church. From every side the people rush in alarm into the Tsaritsa's courtyard, and there find their young prince lying dead, his throat gashed by an assassin's knife. His almost frantic mother accuses Godunof's partisans of the murder. The people seize them, and immediately put them to death.

About twelve hours after the murder was committed, the news reaches the English ambassador, Jerome Horsey, at Yaroslaf. He has been for some days, he writes, in fear of his life, and when, about midnight, he hears a rapping at his gate, he

[7] " Russia in the Sixteenth Century," p. 254.

commends his soul to God. Then he and his servants go to the gate, some fifteen in number, "well furnished with pistolls and weapons." There by the moonlight he sees one of Prince Dimitry's relatives, who hurriedly tells him that the Tsarevich is dead, and his mother "poysoned and upon pointe of death;" adding that her hair and nails are falling off, and crying "Help and geave some good thinge for the passion of Christe his sake." Then Horsey runs to fetch "a littell bottell of pure sallett oyell (that littell vial of balsam that the queen [Elizabeth] gave me) and a box of Venice treacle," and hands them over the wall to his visitor, "who hied him post awaie."

An inquest is held in Uglitch, conducted by Godunof's partisans. They report that the Tsarevich has died from natural causes. The people of Uglitch are punished for their presumption in having dared to lay violent hands on Godunof's retainers. Even the bell on which the alarm was sounded, says tradition, is sent to Siberia. All is perfectly well explained and accounted for: and Boris Godunof may now take his rest, quietly waiting until the sceptre shall drop from the feeble hand of Feodor into his own firm grasp. There is, it is true, a converted Tartar Prince, in whose favour Ivan IV. resigned during one of his more than usually mad intervals, but he leads a poverty-stricken life in a village, and at last becomes blind. The road to royalty lies open before Boris Godunof. Enormously wealthy, able to bring an army of vassals into the field, backed by a strong party among the nobles, enjoying the undivided favour of the clergy, he appears to command all the elements of success.

One, however, is wanting to him: the favour of the people. Adverse reports concerning the death of the young Prince Dimitry have gone abroad, and spread throughout the whole land. In vain does he try to remove the unfavourable impression thus produced. When a conflagration reduces to ashes a great part of Moscow, he generously contributes to the relief of the sufferers, but the common people whisper among themselves that the city has been set on fire by his command, in order that their attention may be diverted from Prince Dimitry's death. When a little later the Khan of the Crimean Tartars invades Russia, and sweeps in triumph close up to Moscow, looking down upon the city, as so many invaders have done, from the neighbouring heights of the Sparrow Hills—although Boris Godunof succeeds in driving away the invader, yet he gains no favour in the eyes of the people, who attribute the inroad to his sinister policy.

On January 7, 1598, Feodor's feeble existence comes to an end, and a few days later his widow enters a convent, and takes the veil. A strange scene ensues. The Council of Boyars, in which Godunof's friends are strong, invites him to mount the throne. He refuses, and a General Assembly is called to decide the question. On the 17th of February the deputies meet for the first time in the Kremlin. They are 474 in number, 99 being ecclesiastics, 272 nobles, land proprietors, government officials, &c., 33 only being deputies from towns, 27 representing the mercantile class, and 16 the common people.[8] Of these the clergy, following the lead of the Patriarch, are devoted to Boris: as also are some of the great nobles and almost all the small landholders, for whom, as well as for the mercantile class, Boris Godunof has done much. It is not to be wondered at that they elect him to fill the vacant throne. But Boris still refuses, begging to be left within the peaceful walls of the monastery to which he has retired for devotional purposes, in which his sister, the late Tsaritsa Irina, has taken the veil. At length, however, the farce comes to an end. Constrained by the objurgations of the Patriarch, the entreaties of the nobles, and the cries of the common people—who

[8] Solovief, viii. 6 ; Kostomarof, i. 592.

throng the courtyard of the monastery, and, being thereto urged by the argument of threats enforced by blows, "against their will, howl like wolves"— Boris at last exclaims: "O Lord God, I am Thy servant; Thy will be done!" And so the sceptre, which has for more than seven centuries been held by the descendants of Rurik, passes into the hands of the representative of a Tartar noble.

As Tsar, Boris governs at first wisely and mildly; attempting to gain the affection of the people, but utterly failing to do so. They still insist upon attributing to him every disaster—even the terrible famine which the failure of the crops in 1602 brings upon the land, when it is said that human flesh is sold in the market-places of Moscow, and its inhabitants die by thousands of starvation. For this disaffection on their part he is to a great extent indebted to the laws by which he has fettered the peasantry of Russia to the soil; thus placing them under that system of serfdom which, after his time, becoming wider and more intense as years go by, will for two centuries and a half do its worst to crush the life out of the common people of Russia.[9] Before long they have their revenge.

It is towards the end of the year 1600 that a vague rumour first begins to spread abroad among

[9] For a further account of Serfdom, see p. 228.

the people that Prince Dimitry is not really dead, that he still lives to claim the sceptre of his father, Ivan the Terrible. At length the rumour reaches the ears of the Tsar, and from that moment his behaviour undergoes a complete change. He becomes moody and suspicious; like his terrible predecessor, perpetually taking precautions against treachery. He organizes an army of spies. Denunciations flow in upon him, and in their train follow tortures and executions. The prisons are full of the victims of his fears; the scaffolds reek with the blood of his real or fancied enemies. Uncertain whether Dimitry be truly dead, he sends for that Prince's mother, the widow of Ivan IV., and privately questions her as to her son's death. She answers that she cannot tell whether he is alive or dead. Whereupon the Tsar orders her to be kept under close restraint, the Tsaritsa, Godunof's wife, angrily flinging a lighted taper in her face.

By this time the rumours which have long been circulating among the people have assumed the form of tidings to all appearance trustworthy. Prince Dimitry, they assert, is now in Poland. It was not he who was buried at Uglitch, but a plebeian substitute, a mere priest's son. And now he is preparing, with Polish aid, to march upon Moscow, and to wrest the sceptre of his ancestors from the hands of the usurper. In vain does Boris protest, and do his best to prove, that the claimant to the throne is no scion of the House of Rurik, but a certain Grigory Otrepief, a runaway member of one of the lower ranks of the ecclesiastical body. The people refuse to believe in his protests, neither will they pay any attention to the curses fulminated against the Claimant by the Tsar's partisan, the Patriarch. In vain do Boris Godunof's troops vanquish those of his rival. The Tsar is obliged to acknowledge the existence of a vast force, standing like an inexhaustible reserve at the back of his temporarily discomfited antagonist, in the shape of a people's stubborn faith.

Almost distracted by his fears, Boris at one time appeals to warlocks and diviners, at another spends whole days in solitude, sending his son meanwhile to offer up prayers in the churches. One of his last efforts is an attempt to rid himself of his rival by poison. But the monks to whom he entrusts the commission are seized by the enemy before they can execute it.

On the 13th of April, 1605, the Tsar, who is in unusually good spirits, eats a hearty meal, and then ascends to an upper chamber from which he is wont to survey the whole city. Suddenly he descends, complaining of illness. His doctor is hurriedly sent for. By the time he comes the Tsar is senseless, blood streaming from his nose and ears. In the course of the afternoon he dies.

For a time his death is concealed from the people, but next day they are summoned to the Kremlin, in order to "kiss the cross" or swear allegiance to Boris's widow, Maria, and to her son Fedor, a youth sixteen years old. The ceremony is performed quietly, but a few days later the commanders of the royal forces begin to conspire against the new Tsar ; and on the 7th of May, the army goes over to the side of the claimant. On June 1, a vast crowd gathers outside the Kremlin to listen to a proclamation purporting to be issued by the Tsar Dimitry Ivanovich. A great tumult arises. Prince Shouisky, who conducted the inquest at Uglitch at the time of the supposed murder, is sent for, and questioned as to what then took place. He replies : " Boris ordered Dimitry to be killed, but the Tsarevich was saved. The son of a priest was buried in his place." Then the crowd, shouting " Hail, Dimitry Ivanovich!" and "Down with the Godunofs!" rushes into the Kremlin, and bursts into the palace. The young monarch is sitting on the throne ; his mother and sister standing by his side with holy pictures in their hands. The people do them no injury, merely placing them under restraint; but a few days later, two boyars of Dimitry's party arrive in Moscow, and by their orders the Tsar and his mother are killed. Their deaths, as well as that of the late Tsar, are attributed to suicide by poison, so their bodies are buried without funeral rites. And in the same grave with them is placed the coffin containing the remains of Boris Godunof, which have been dug up from their place in the cathedral in which the dead Tsars of Russia are privileged to repose.

There are few chapters of history stranger than that which relates the short-lived success of the enigmatical personage generally known by the name of the False Demetrius. Very little that is certain is known of his early career, previous to the time when we find him asserting that he is the Prince Dimitry, whom murderous hands are said to have done to death at Uglitch, and asking for aid from Poland to enable him to mount his father's throne. In March, 1604, he is kindly received at Cracow by King Sigismund III., and placed in the hands of Jesuit teachers. A few months later, having accepted the hard conditions imposed upon him for their own advantage by the king, the Jesuits, and George Mniszek, the Palatine of Sandomir, to whose daughter Marina he is engaged to be married, he sets out on what might appear to be a foolhardy expedition against the reigning Tsar of Russia. But around him gathers an army comprising all that is most bold, and adventurous, and reckless in what is now South Russia: his forces daily increase as he proceeds, and when he has crossed the Russian frontier, town after town accepts his claim to sovereignty, and before long a considerable portion of Russia owns his sway. At last the army declares in his favour, and on June 20, 1605, he enters the capital in triumph, amid the acclamations of the assembled population. A month later arrives the widow of Ivan IV., the mother of Prince Demetrius. The new monarch, who has postponed his coronation till she can grace it by her presence, goes forth to meet her, followed by a vast assemblage of inquisitive spectators. When her litter stops, and she draws back its curtain, the Tsar leaps from his horse and flings himself into her arms. With sobbing and with tears a mutual recognition takes place in the sight of all the people. Then the widowed Tsaritsa is borne into Moscow in her litter, by the side of which walks the Tsar, amid the clanging of church bells, and the joyous cries of the populace, in whose minds not a shadow of doubt now lingers as to their ruler's identity.

M

Dimitry's coronation takes place on July 30, and with it a new and happy era appears to have dawned for Russia. The Tsar shows himself the direct reverse of what Ivan the Terrible and Boris Godunof have been. Merciful, kindly, genial, tolerant in religious matters, friendly towards education and general enlightenment, a foe to spies and informers, he seems to be about to bestow priceless blessings on the Russian land. But his indifference, or even hostility on Church questions, displeases the clergy, and his Polish retainers give great offence to the people, who look with little favour also upon his Polish wife Marina, to whom he is married on the 8th of May, 1605. While the wedding festivities are being celebrated, a party of conspirators are preparing to assassinate the Tsar. Prince Shouisky is its leader, with whom are joined a number of other nobles to whom the new court is obnoxious. Tidings of their intentions are brought to the Tsar, but he refuses to listen to them, continuing his revels in full reliance upon the affectionate fidelity of his subjects.

About four o'clock in the morning of the 16th of May one of the church bells begins to clang, and in a short time all the belfries of Moscow are sounding an alarm. The conspirators have seized all the gates of the Kremlin, and by means of a false order have got rid of the greater part of its guards. When the people come rushing into the open space in front of the Kremlin walls, eager to know what is the meaning of the alarm, they are told that the Poles are attacking the boyars, and intend to kill the Tsar, whereupon they immediately rush off to attack those unsuspecting foreigners. Then with a drawn sword in one hand, and a cross in the other, Prince Shouisky enters the Kremlin, followed by the armed conspirators.

Aroused by the clang of bells, the Tsar at first believes what one of the conspirators tells him, that a fire has broken out in the city. But presently he sees the armed array of Shouisky's followers advancing, and too late the truth flashes upon his mind. After a vain attempt to defend the palace, he sees that his only chance of escape depends upon his being able to make his way to where the people are crowding together on the other side of the Kremlin walls. Outside his palace stands some wooden scaffolding, erected at the time of the wedding illuminations. He rushes into his wife's chamber, and calls to her to save herself, then, leaping from one of the windows upon the woodwork, he tries to escape along it. But the attempt fails. He falls from the scaffolding to the ground, a height of thirty feet.

There he is found by some of his guards, who carry him, seriously injured, into the palace. The conspirators rush in, and all now depends upon the fidelity of the soldiers. Dimitry promises them rich rewards if they will save him. Shouisky threatens to slay their wives and children if they will not surrender the Tsar. At length they reply that they will give him up if the Tsaritsa Maria, Prince Dimitry's mother, repudiates him; but if she still maintains that he is her son, they will die in his cause. Prince Ivan Golitsyn is sent to put the question to the Tsaritsa. Presently he returns, and affirms that she says that her son was killed in Uglitch, and that this man is an impostor. Her alleged words are repeated to the people, with the addition that the Tsar himself has confessed to his imposition. In a moment the popular feeling sets against its late favourite, and a few minutes later, his naked corpse is being dragged out of the Kremlin to the Red Square. For some time it lies there exposed to public view, a mask attached to its breast, the chanter of a bagpipe applied to its mouth.[1] Then it is buried in the "House of the Poor," the "Strangers' Field" devoted to the remains of the poor and friendless. But before long, rumours begin to spread among the people

[1] Symbols of the sorcery of which he was accused.

that his sorceries are the cause of the prevailing frosts, that his corpse walks vampire-like by nights. So they rush in crowds to the cemetery, disinter his remains, and consume them with fire. His ashes, mixed with gunpowder, are fired from a gun, pointed in the direction of the road by which he entered Moscow.

Marina, who for so short a time filled the position of Tsaritsa, is represented in popular tradition as having escaped from the Kremlin in the shape of a magpie. For in the memory of the people, her name still lives as that of an heretical or infidel magician. In reality, on the terrible night of the 16th of May, she evaded the first rush of her foes, taking refuge beneath the hooped petticoat of one of her ladies in waiting. Afterwards she was put under restraint, but not unkindly treated.

To the throne, left vacant by the death of Dimitry, succeeds Vassily Shouisky: his election being ratified by the voice of the Moscow people, called together by his partizans for that purpose, but not being submitted to any General Assembly of the nation. Then follows the "troublous period" of Russian history, during which appears a swarm of pretenders, one saying he is a son of Ivan IV., another claiming as his father that

Tsarevich Ivan whom Ivan IV. killed, but most of them giving themselves out to be sons of Tsar Feodor. One of these, calling himself the Tsarevich Peter Feodorovich, obtains a considerable following, but at length he is taken and hanged in Tula. The others, for the most part, figure but a short time in history. At last, however, there comes upon the stage a pretender who for a considerable period maintains his claims. Stating that he is the Tsar Dimitry, escaped from the hands of Shouisky and his fellow conspirators, he sets up his camp in Tushino, a few miles from Moscow, and calls upon the nation to acknowledge him as its rightful monarch. And a great part of the nation does so acknowledge him: besides which his claims are supported by an army of Polish and other volunteers. In the autumn of 1608, Marina, the widow of the first "False Demetrius," is brought into his camp. At first, it is said, she refuses to acknowledge him, but at last, yielding to the expostulations of her father, who has been bought over, she consents to confirm the story of the second "False Demetrius," and to recognize him in public as her lawful spouse. Before long it seems as if the voice of the entire nation is about to summon the pretender to the throne.[2]

[2] Who he really was, is uncertain. Various accounts (says

Shouisky in utter despair turns for help to Sweden. By this time, Moscow, and indeed almost all the northern part of the Muscovite realm, is in the hands of the "Tushino Rogue," as the Pretender is called. Only the great monastery of the Troitsa, a fortified town in itself, holds forth bravely against a besieging army, at first comprising some threescore thousand Poles and other enemies, and afterwards some ten thousand, while the besieged cannot muster more than fifteen hundred men capable of bearing arms, besides peasants and monastery servants. For sixteen months lasts the siege. Then the Poles on January 12, 1610, retire from before the Troitsa walls. For by this time Prince Skopin-Shouisky, one of the few real patriots of that degraded age, is at hand with a strong force of both Russian and Swedish troops. On the 12th of March he enters Moscow in triumph, received with reverent joy as their preserver by the almost despairing inhabitants.

Before this takes place, the Pretender, finding his army melting away, has retired from Tushino to

Kostomarof i, 641) describe him as (1) a Lithuanian named Bogdan, (2) a Jew, (3) a converted Jew, (4) a son of Prince Kurbsky, (5) a man from Kief sent by the priest Vorobei, (6) a foreigner sent into Russia by Mniszek's wife, (7) a Starodub man, successively schoolmaster in Shklof and in Mohilef.

Kaluga ; on the 15th of March his fortified camp, which has so long been threatening Moscow, is burnt by its occupants. The Tsar's prospects now appear to be clearing : but just as Russia begins to come back to its allegiance, the Polish king Sigismund declares war, and besieges Smolensk. Towards the end of April, also, Prince Skopin-Shouisky, to whom all faithful Russian eyes turn with gratitude, looking upon him as the saver of the country in its hour of direst need, is taken ill at a banquet, and soon after dies—poisoned, say the people, by the direction of the jealous Tsar.

Vassily Shouisky's fall is now imminent. On June 23 a Polish army utterly defeats the Russian troops, and its leader, Zolkiewski, marches straight upon Moscow. At the same time the Pretender leaves Kaluga, and on July 11 arrives within a short distance of the capital. On the 17th Shouisky is obliged to abdicate, and two days later he is forced, vainly protesting, into the monastic order.

Thus ends the brief reign of the last direct descendant of Rurik, who sat upon the Russian throne.[3] A short time before his dethronement, say the Moscow people, in the Church of the Archangel in the Kremlin, where rest the remains

[3] He was directly descended from St. Vladimir, sixteen steps intervening.

of the Tsars his kinsmen, there was heard at midnight a sound of wailing. Then a voice read out the hundred and eighteenth psalm, and a requiem was sung. With wailing began the ghostly service, with wailing did it end : foreboding the coming fall of the family which for more than seven centuries had ruled the Russian people, the many sorrows which were still destined to come upon the Russian land.

After long disputes and much confusion, King Sigismund's son, Ladislas, is at last accepted as Tsar by the Moscow Council of Nobles, the consent of the nation not being asked, and on the 19th of September a Polish army enters the capital. In December, the Pretender, the Tushino or Kaluga Rogue as he is called, is killed by some of his attendants, and all things seem to favour the partizans of Ladislas. But Sigismund shows himself discontented with the conditions imposed upon his son, and he presses on the siege of Smolensk. Now that the Pretender is no longer to be feared, the adherents of Ladislas begin to fall off in their devotion to that prince. The orthodoxy of the nation is shocked at the thought that a schismatic is sitting upon the throne. From town to town, and from village to village, spreads a feeling of dissatisfaction, gradually strengthening into a burning indignation against the insolent foreigners who have undertaken to rule and to vex Holy Russia, into a vehement desire to sweep them from off the face of the land and to live again in peace under a Russian monarch. The severe and stubborn Patriarch Hermogenes feeds the flame of the nation's wrath, organizing an armed rising throughout the country. In a short time the troops of twenty-five cities take the field under the command of Procopy Liapunof. In the beginning of March, 1611, they set out for Moscow, and towards the end of the month they invest it on every side. Meanwhile the capital undergoes terrible sufferings. As soon as the Poles who garrison it hear that the country is in revolt against Ladislas, they begin to maltreat the citizens among whom they have hitherto lived peaceably. In a short time the city becomes a scene of bloodshed and destruction. A quarrel arises one day between some Polish soldiers, and a number of Russian carters, whom they order to assist in dragging artillery to the ramparts. A vast crowd collects. Suddenly the foreigners fall upon the unarmed natives, of whom upwards of 7000 are killed in the Kitai-Gorod. But in the Bély-Gorod, or White Town, the Muscovites defend themselves vigorously, fighting behind hastily-constructed barricades, and flinging missiles from their roofs and windows. Then the Poles set the city on fire, a strong wind arises, and before long the whole of the White Town is in a blaze. All night long rages the conflagration. At length nothing remains of Moscow but the parts held by the Poles, the Kremlin and the Kitai-Gorod, or China-Town. During a terrible frost the homeless fugitives from the burning city are obliged to wander about the open country, too often vainly seeking for shelter.

Again the prospects of Russia darken. Early in June Smolensk is taken by storm, and Sigismund threatens to overrun the whole country. The Swedish troops, who were originally called in by Vassily Shouisky to act against the Poles, now begin to seize the northern towns, Novgorod included, in the name of their own king. In Pskof a new "False Demetrius" appears; while several districts are swearing allegiance to the son of Marina by the "Tushino Rogue," the second "False Demetrius." The south is being ravaged by the Crimean Tartars. Over the whole face of the land wander troops of highwaymen and brigands.

But still a firm determination not to yield exists among the Russian cities, greatly strengthened by the exhortations of the Church, which now supports the courage of the down-trodden people in their struggle for national existence against the forces of the "schismatic" west, as it has supported it before during the long and gloomy years in which Russia groaned under the power of the "pagan" East. As Alexis and Sergius succeeded in binding together in powerful alliance the scattered and jarring elements of Russian strength, so does Dionysius, the Archimandrite of the Troitsa monastery, now succeed in persuading the nobles and the municipalities of Russia to bestir themselves and act in unison in behalf of their endangered religion and their afflicted fatherland. A report spreads abroad that a heavenly vision has been vouchsafed to a godly man in Nijny Novgorod. Two mystic elders have appeared to him in a dream, and have declared that Russia cannot be saved until its people repent and are cleansed of their sins. Therefore let them fast for three days, and so prepare themselves to receive heavenly aid. And the fast, it is said, is rigidly kept throughout the whole land, and then a thrill of expectation and of hope stirs every loyal Russian heart.

However this may be, we see in October, 1611, a General Assembly held in Nijny Novgorod. The sound of the great cathedral bell calls all the

anxious citizens together. After divine service
the protopope addresses the people assembled outside the cathedral, exhorts them to stand fast by
their holy faith, and reads to them a summons to
action just received from the Troitsa monastery.
Then comes forward the famous flesher Minin,[4] and
appeals to his hearers to submit to any sacrifices
rather than to allow the national cause to languish
for want of means, even if they have to sell their
homesteads, and to borrow money on the security
of their wives and children. His enthusiasm proves
contagious ; his hearers respond to his call. In a
little time an armed revolt is organized, Minin
directing the provision of resources, Prince Dimitry
Pojarsky assuming the military command. Before
long we see a Russian army take the field,
march triumphantly upon Moscow, and in August,
1612, lay siege to the capital. The Poles are soon
reduced to great straits. At length, after undergoing terrible sufferings from famine, and even
supporting themselves for some time, it is said, on
human flesh, the foreign garrison is obliged to
yield[5].

[4] Kozma Zacharych Minin-Sukhoruk.
[5] It is to this period of famine that the very improbable
story is referred of a judge being obliged to leap from his
seat and rush out of court, in order to escape from being
seized and eaten by the prisoners at the bar.

With the 25th of October, 1612,[6] longsuffering Moscow at length sees a joyful day arrive. The Russian troops enter the Kremlin, preceded by a solemn procession of clergy, bearing holy pictures and crosses, the Archimandrite Dionysius at their head. And from the Kremlin comes to meet them the Archbishop of Archangel, bearing in his hands the famous Vladimir picture of the Virgin, so dear to all Russian eyes.

In a short time Russia is once more free; for Sigismund and his son Ladislas make but a slight attempt to renew their claims. About Christmas the Russian towns receive orders to send up deputies to a General Assembly about to be held at Moscow for the election of a new Tsar. It assembles, and on the 21st of February, 1613, its final meeting is held; its choice falling on Michael, the young son of Fedor Nikitich Romanof, known in religion as Filaret, Metropolitan of Rostof. The young Romanof, who is but sixteen years old, at first refuses the proffered honour—an honour which the events of the last few years have deprived of

[6] There is some confusion among the historians as to this date. Kostomarof fixes it as the 25th of October. Solovief says November 27, distinctly stating, moreover, that the Kremlin held out a month after the Kitai-Gorod fell on October 22.

much of its usual charm. But at length he consents to gratify the wish of the people, and on the 11th of July, 1613, he is crowned Tsar of Russia.

Since that day the house of Romanof has ruled the Russian land. Michael's grandson became world-renowned as the Emperor Peter the Great, the creator of a new Russia. And throughout all time will be remembered, as the Liberator of the long-enslaved masses of the Russian people, Peter's great-grandson's grandson, the Emperor Alexander the Second.

CHAPTER VII.

SUPPLEMENTARY.

THE preceding chapters having been devoted to narrative, I have hitherto abstained, as a general rule, from anything like criticism. Authorities have seldom been quoted, and differences of opinion among Russian historians have, to some extent, been ignored. I now propose to return to the point from which we started, and to string together a few critical notes, extracted from Russian books, which may serve to illustrate and explain some of the more dubious passages in the story which we have heard related, and to place upon record the opinions respecting that story which the most recent historians of Russia entertain. I will take

I.—THE OLD SLAVONIANS.

As regards the area occupied in olden times by the Slavonic family—a painful subject to many

Slavonic writers, who hold that the Teutonic races have always been attempting to oust or crush the Slavic—let us take the first of the maps in an atlas published at St. Petersburg by E. Zamyslovsky[1] which professes to represent Eastern and Central Europe between the years 862 and 1054. On it we see the western boundary of the Slavonic world defined by a line drawn from a point on the river Eyder not far distant from the present Kiel to the head of the Adriatic. Thence it follows the east coast of the Adriatic as far as Scutari, then skirts the territory of the Albanians, crosses Macedonia and Thrace, bends northwards near Adrianople, and strikes the Black Sea somewhat below the mouth of the Danube. Following the coast of the Black Sea to the north of the Boug, it runs for some distance along the west bank of that river, and then shoots northwards to the river Ros, following its course till the Dnieper is reached. Along the Dnieper it runs as far as the river Psel, which it follows nearly to its source. Thence it diverges in a north-east direction, crosses the Don, and soon afterwards sweeps in a sinuous curve north-westwards to Lake Ladoga. Thence it bends to the west and south, skirting the territories, along

[1] Uchebny Atlas po Russkoi Istorii, 1869.

the Gulf of Finland and the Baltic, occupied by the Finnish races as far as the mouth of the Dvina, and by the Lettic as far as the mouth of the Vistula. Then from about Dantzic to Kiel it follows the Baltic coast. Almost the whole of the vast space contained within this boundary line, with the exception of the districts held by the Hungarians and Wallachians, is coloured green, on the map to show that it is occupied by a Slavonic race. In the eastern and northern parts, however, of what is now Russia, the Finnish element is strong.

If we now take that part of the Slavonic world in which we are more particularly interested, we find in the neighbourhood of Lake Ilmen and down the Volkhof to Lake Ladoga, the settlements of the *Slaviane*; along the (western) Dvina and the upper part of the Dnieper live the *Krivichi*, part of whom are known as *Polochane*. From the Berezina to the Pripet and the Pinsk Marshes dwell the *Driagovichi;* between the Dnieper and the Sozh are the *Rodimichi;* along the Dnieper, from the junction of the Pripet to that of the Ros, are the *Poliane;* to their north-west live the *Drevliane;* and north-eastwards, on the other side of the Dnieper, the *Séveriane*. To the east of these tribes are the *Viatichi*, and a number of Slavonic colonies scattered among a Finnish population. Outside these "Russian"

Slavs[2]—to the north and north-east are settled divers Finnish peoples; to the south-east and south roam various races of apparently Turkish origin, the Bulgarians on the Oka and the Volga, and the Khazars, whose territories extend from the lower part of the Volga to the Dnieper.[3] To the west, the northern or Lake Ilmen Slavs have as their neighbours the Finnish inhabitants of what is now Livonia and Esthonia; the territories of the *Krivichi*, the *Polochane*, and the *Driagovichi* are bounded by *Litva*—the home of the Lithuanians. Letts, Old Prussians, and other kindred tribes (including perhaps the doubtful race of the *Yatviagi*), who form one of the two divisions (the Slavs forming the other), into which the Letto-Slavic branch of the Aryan family seems to have split after its separation from the Teutonic branch. But westwards of the *Drevliane* and *Poliane*, and their immediate neighbours, the *Volyniane, Bujane*, &c., no alien possessions break the continuity of Slavonic occupation, till the Lower Elbe or the mountains of the Boehmerwald are reached, the whole of the land being held by various Slavonic races:—Poles, Czekhs, Moravians, Slovaks, Croatians, and the numerous peoples known to

[2] That is to say, Slavs living in what is now Russia.
[3] Bestujef-Riumin, i., chap. i. p. 6.

the Germans by the general designation of Wends.[4]

Of the religion of the Slavs in general we know very little, and for that scanty amount we are almost entirely dependent upon the doubtful evidence of alien and hostile witnesses; of that of the Russian Slavs in particular we are singularly ignorant.[5] Nor do we know much more about their manners and customs. Of the *Poliane* the chronicle known as Nestor's says, " Every man lived in his own *rod* separately, on his own ground : every man ruled his own *rod.*" The word *rod* is now technically employed in the sense of "association of relatives" or clan ; and therefore some writers hold that the Slavs originally formed clans, and that it was in this clannish state that they were found by their Varangian visitors. But others maintain that the Slavs formed not clans but family communities ; for the word *rod* originally meant family [*rodìt'* or *rajdàt'* = to beget], just as the modern word for family, *sem'ya*, originally meant wife ;[6] and,

---

[4] A good description of the Wends of the present day, as well as an account of their predecessors, will be found in R. Andree's *Wendische Wanderstudien.* Stuttgart, 1874.

[5] I have attempted to give some information about its leading divinities in the " Songs of the Russian People," pp. 80—103.

[6] "*Sem'ya* [says Solovief, i. p. 317. Note 47] (from *so-*

therefore, all that the old chronicler intended to say was that every man was the head of his own household.

Bestujef-Riumin [i. chap. i. p. 43, &c.] considers that Slavonic society had as its foundation the "family-community, united partly by common descent, but still more by common living together, by tilling of the ground in common, and by its own dispensation of justice within its own boundaries." A cluster of these family communities formed what among the western Slavs was called a *jupa* (the Russian *volost* or *pogost*), a species of district or hundred. At the head of the *jupa* was the personage styled the *jupan*—a title answering to the old Slavonic *kniaz*, which now means prince. In the centre of the *jupa* stood the *grad* (*gorod*), or town, its religious as well as political centre; for in it were religious rites performed and sacrifices offered up. No special class of priests, however, appears to have existed among the eastern Slavs. Over the face of the land were dotted small vil-

---

imayu) [*con-habeo*] originally stood for *zhena, supruga* (*sopryagayu, so-imayu*) [*spryagát'* = to yoke together horses, to conjugate verbs], but was afterwards applied also to the offspring arising from *suprujestvo* or co-habitation. Wives used to be accustomed to subscribe their letters to their husbands, ' thy *Sem'itsa* So-and-So'."

lages, consisting of miserable wooden huts. To this day, says Andree, the villages of the Wends in Lusatia may be distinguished by their smallness from those of their German neighbours.

The Slavs, of whom history makes no mention in a nomad state, were an agricultural people,[7] and therefore of a peaceable nature. It was only among the Baltic Slavonians that their chief gods assumed a warlike character. Buslaef thinks that the fact of the Slavs having counted by summers, instead of by winters, evinces a softness of character as compared with the ferocity of their German and Scandinavian neighbours.

The Slavs seem really to have been a comparatively mild people, although (as is stated above at p. 4) parents in some of the tribes were allowed to kill their daughters.[8] But they fought boldly in the

[7] The Germans, who generally despised the Slavs, admitted they were good tillers of the soil. St. Boniface, the Apostle of Germany, who described them as " fœdissimum et deterrimum genus hominum," employed them to colonize the neighbourhoods of Fulda, Bamberg, Wurtzburg, &c. Grimm thinks the word *pflug*, plough, may have been borrowed from the Slavonic *plug*. Dahl, on the other hand, in his great dictionary classes *plug* among the words of German origin.

[8] " Si plures filias aliqua genuisset, ut ceteris facilius providerent, aliquas ex eis jugulabant, pro nichilo ducentes parricidium," is said of some of the Baltic Slavs by Herbordus in his "Vita Ottonis" (Pertz, M. G. H. Scriptores. xii. 794).

field, surrounding themselves when attacked by a rampart of linked cars, with their wives and children in the middle; just as in later days the Hussites used to defend themselves in their tabors or field-camps. They for a long time fought only on foot; but a "survival" from a period in which they may have led a nomad and horse-riding life, may perhaps be recognized in the custom of setting their boys on horseback when eight years old, the time also for cutting their flowing locks.[9] Such appears to have been the state of society among Lake Ilmen Slavs when the Varangians first came among them.

II.—THE VARANGIANS.[1]

Who these Varangians were still remains a moot point. Bestujef-Riumin [i. c. i. p. 88—96] divides the present authorities on the subject into three principal schools:—the first asserting the Scandinavian origin of the Varangians, the second tracing

[9] Bestujef-Riumin [i. chap. i. p. 63] looks upon this mounting on horseback as a later rite, on the ground that the Slavs long fought on foot. But it may have always been due to a reminiscence of an older period, as probably was the religious rite of horse-flesh eating among the thoroughly pedestrian Northmen.

[1] See above, p. 13. I have adopted the usual spelling. The Russians write *Variagi*.

them to Slavonic territories along the Baltic, the third seeing in them an armed fraternity of mixed nationality. The first theory is maintained almost universally out of Russia,[2] and therefore there is no great necessity to dwell on it here. Of the second, or Slavonic school,[3] the earliest champion was the famous Lomonosof. Among the upholders of the third theory is the historian Solovief [i. 104], who thinks that we may deduce from what has been written on the subject "the firm conviction that under the name of Variagi are to be understood Drujinas (or armed companies) formed of men who have voluntarily or involuntarily left their fatherland, and have become obliged to seek their fortune

[2] Mr. Hyde Clark denies that the Varangians were Scandinavians. He identifies them with the Varini—a race connected with the Angli who settled in England.

[3] Its chief productions, says Bestujef-Riumin, are Yury Venelin's *Skandinavomaniya*, Moscow, 1845; I. V. Savelief-Rostislawich's *Slav. Sbornik* ["Slavonic Collection"], Petersburg, 1845; F. L. Moroshkin's *O Znachenii imeni Rusof i Slavyan* [on the meaning of the names Russi and Slaviane], Petersburg, 1841; M. A. Maksimovich's *Otkuda idet Russkaya Zemlya* [Whence comes the Russian Land], 1837, &c. Especially important are some critical articles by S. A. Gedeonof and N. J. Nadejdin in various periodical publications. One good service rendered by the school, according to Bestuyef-Riumin is the enforcement of a greater precision in the use of the word *Rus*, which is now applied only to the Kief or mid-Dnieper district.

at sea or in foreign parts." Lamansky and Pogodin appear to be of the same opinion, to which Bestujef-Riumin seems also to incline : namely, that the Varangians were a warlike body of men, composed of various nationalities, but in which the Scandinavian element preponderated ; a body from which the Emperor's guard at Constantinople was recruited, and which on that account was kept in constant connexion with the lands occupied by the Slavs about Lake Ilmen and along the Dnieper, the inhabitants of the highway leading from the hungry North to the rich fields of the Byzantine Empire.[4]

It was in 859, according to Nestor's Chronicle, that the Varangians came from beyond the sea, and exacted tribute from the Northern Slavs and their

[4] Bestujef-Riumin refers also to the opinion of Ewers and Neumann deducing the Varangians from the shores of the Black Sea. Kostomarof [i. p. 11, note] says, " Variagi (Varingiar) was the name borne by the inhabitants of the Scandinavian peninsulas," who took service with the Byzantine Emperors, and journeyed from their native land to Greece across Russia by water, making use of the rivers between the Baltic and the Black Sea. ·As they represented Scandinavia in the eyes of the Russians, their designation became used in Russia as a general term for all the inhabitants of Scandinavia, and eventually for all West-Europeans—just as every Western European is now called by the Russian peasantry a *Nyemets* or German.

Finnish neighbours. The date is merely approximative. The important fact is that there seems to have been some sort of a confederation in the neighbourhood of Lake Ilmen, and that the Baltic "armed bands" fell upon them (probably by no means for the first time), and rendered them tributary. Equally approximative is the date of 862 ascribed to the arrival of Rurik [see above, p. 13]. From that time till the death of Vladimir I. lasts

III.—THE VARANGIAN PERIOD.

Of this period Kostomarof draws a very gloomy picture. Till the introduction of Christianity, he justly says, the history of Russia is shrouded in dense obscurity. For the chroniclers did not begin to write until the second half of the eleventh century, and for the events preceding that time they had no better sources of information, with the exception of a few Byzantine annals, than the dubious legends preserved among the people by oral tradition. Even the story which relates how Christianity was introduced into Russia rests upon somewhat feeble evidence. The zealous monks who compiled it, wrote at a time when the new religion had everywhere, except in a few outlying districts, displaced the old. And they seem, not unnaturally, to have done everything which lay in their power to darken the characters of the heathen Olga, the heathen Vladimir—in order to bring out in clear relief against their gloomy backgrounds the brightness of the forms under which they have depicted Olga and Vladimir, the Christian and the Holy.

Præ-Christian Russia, according to the same historian (p. 3), was in a miserable condition. Its Slavonic tribes were disunited, without common interests, wielding no concentrated power. Rurik and his successors till the time of Vladimir's conversion, did scarcely anything for the land: the princes and their armed companies caring for nothing but plunder, and behaving like mere pirates or marauders. Some good influence was no doubt brought to bear on the Russian Slavs during their time by Byzantium and the Arabian East: but it was Christianity which really civilized and consolidated the land—throughout which, after Vladimir's conversion, it spread with singular rapidity, there being no priestly class to oppose it or excite the people against it.

Other writers take a less dismal view of the Varangian Period. As regards the beneficent influence of Christianity all are quite in unison with Kostomarof. But they do not seem to see in

Vladimir's predecessors the utter barbarians whom that excellent but not easily satisfied historian describes.

There is little doubt that the early princes thought more about their own interests than those of the land they governed, identified themselves more with their drujinas (or bands of military retainers) than with the mass of their peaceable subjects. From the earliest times we see the prince surrounded by a body of men who follow him as warriors to the field, and assist him by their advice in the council-chamber at home. This body of retainers, or "court-men," is called the prince's *drujina* (from *drug*, a friend). Its highest members are *boyare;*[5] besides these are the *gridi*,[6] after whom the prince's council chamber is called the *gridnitsa*. The general term for its members is *muji*, or men; when applied as a special designation, that name refers to the lower class of the *drujina*. The *drujina* is composed of men of various nationalities, but at first Scandinavians are probably in the majority.

[5] The word *Boyarin* (plural *boyare*) was long supposed to be of foreign origin, but Srezniefsky traces it to Slavonic roots : *boi* (or *voi*), battle to.

[6] Said to be identical with the Icelandic *Hirðmenn*. But *Grid* is also claimed as a Slavonic word : in one dialect *grida* means a gathering of people, crowd, &c.

In case of war, besides the *drujina*, the *voï*, or "forces," are called out. At their head is the *voevoda* [*vodit'* = to lead]. In order to guard the frontiers, towns are built in which picked men of various nationalities are placed. The frontier itself appears to have been guarded by some sort of a wall.

Separate from the *muji* or men forming the princely *drujina* are the *liudi* [folks, *leute*], the lowest class of whom are known as *smerdui*. There are also *gosti* [guests, i. e. merchants], but they do not form anything like a caste. A merchant can become a warrior at will, and be received into the prince's *drujina* if he desires it. The only strong line of social demarcation is that which divides the freeman from the slave [*kholop* or *rab*], who appears to have been generally a captive taken in war.[7]

We have seen that Kostomarof justly discredits many of the accounts of the heathen princes of Russia, written long after their time by Christian monks. The only evidence, therefore, in confirmation of his unfavourable opinion of those princes is looked upon by himself with reasonable suspicion. I do not think we need agree with him in designating their period as one of "complete bar-

[7] This sketch is abridged from chap. ii. of Bestujef-Riumin's History, pp. 108—118, compared with Solovief, i. 237—259.

barism." They were probably not unlike the heathen chieftains of whom we read in Icelandic sagas—decidedly not perfect, but with very many good points about them. From these sagas, in all probability, a number of the early Russian traditions have been borrowed. The first Varangian princes probably brought their own scalds or sagamen with them from Scandinavia, who would convey the traditions of their northern home to the shores of Lake Ilmen and the banks of the Dnieper. We may take as examples the legends of Oleg and of Olga, related above at pp. 17 and 21. The artifice ascribed to Olga, that of obtaining birds from a besieged town, and letting them fly with burning rags attached to them, so as to set the town on fire, is attributed in the "Heimskringla Saga" to Harald Hardrada. It is true that he lived long after Olga's time, but he died, in all probability, before the monastic Chronicler composed his account of Olga's life. The legend of Oleg's death, caused by a serpent which glides out of the skull of the steed against which he has been warned, is more manifestly a borrowed tale. In order to be convinced of this, we have only to compare it with the Icelandic saga of Oddr.

In it Oddr, surnamed of the Arrows—for he possesses magic arrows which, like Indra's lance or

Thor's hammer, fly to their mark and then return
to their master's hand, missiles which at once invest their possessor with a mythological character
—is told by the prophetess Herda, that he will
live 300 years, and then be stung to death by a
serpent which will issue from the head of Faxi, his
steed. So he slays Faxi, and heaps a mound over
its remains. Many a year passes by. He marries
the daughter of the King of ,Gardarike (i. e. Russia),
and in good time succeeds to his throne. At
length, however, he visits his native land. There,
one day, he comes to a tempest-bared spot, and
sees something dry and old and white. " Is it not
a horse's head ?" he cries. " Is it not Faxi's head?"
and so saying he strikes the skull of Faxi, for such
it really is ; and from out of the skull shoots an
adder and stings the heel of the king. Then Oddr
sings his death-song : and his followers burn his
body, and bear back the mournful tidings to his
widowed Russian Queen. Solovief [i. 345, note 187]
identifies Oddr with Oleg ; but as the legend is connected also with our own Isle of Sheppey, not to
mention other places, such identification appears
to be hazardous. Pushkin has versified the Russian tradition, and the English variant figures
among the Ingoldsby Legends.

As cautiously as these prose legends—looking

upon them from a historian's point of view—must be handled the poems preserved in the memory of the people, which profess to sing the glories of Kief during the reign of the great Vladimir. They are invaluable to the student of folk-lore and comparative mythology, and interesting in the highest degree as waifs and strays from the great mass of popular poetry which has suffered shipwreck on the stream of time. Well worthy are they of the conscientious and intelligent care bestowed upon collecting them by Ruibnikof, the Kiréefskys, and that martyr to his enthusiasm in their cause, the lamented Alexander Hilferding. But the metrical romances or *builinas* belonging to the " Vladimir Cycle " can scarcely be said to throw any historic light upon the character of the princely Christianizer of Russia.[8] As little can we gleam from the *builinas* about the actual ruler of Kief at the close of the Varangian Period, as we can gather from the Morte d'Arthur about any real Prince of the Silures, or from the chronicle of the Pseudo-Turpin concerning a genuine battle of Roncesvalles.

IV.—THE APPANAGE PERIOD.

With the death of Yaroslaf I. commences this

[8] Or upon that of Vladimir Monomachus, to whom also they have been supposed to apply.

period, fraught with so many woes to Russia. How the *udyelui*,⁹ or separate principalities arose, and what was their exact influence on the fortunes of the land of which they formed the component parts, are still vexed questions—the cause in Russia of a considerable amount of discussion. The following are the opinions of the chief authorities :—

The earlier Russian historians, including Karamzin, supposed that the division of Russia into appanages was due to the moral weakness of its Princes, who were injudiciously attached to their children, and favoured them at the expense of their subjects.

Polevoi suggests that the system may have been due to an imaginary development of feudal ideas. Nadejdin, correctly discerning that the appanage and the feudal systems had nothing in common, comes to the conclusion that we must look for the full explanation of the fact that Russia was subdivided in the patrimonial customs of the Slavonic peoples.

Pogodin traces the cause of the formation of appanages to the common right of the princely families to rule the land which their fathers and

---

⁹ *Dyelit'* = to divide, to *deal. Udyelit'* = to deal out or utterly, to assign, give, &c. *Udyel* = part assigned, share, &c.

grandfathers had won. For all the appanaged princes claimed to be descendants of Rurik.

Solovief is of a somewhat similar opinion, though he bases the claims of those princes on the old *rodovoi buit* or clannish mode of life.

The fact that similar appanage systems existed in other lands peopled by Slavonic races seems to confirm the last hypothesis. It is maintained by the majority of Russian scholars, but of late years various protests have been made against it. Thus Passek attributes the prevalence of appanages less to the mutual relations of the princes than to the striving after independence of the civic communities. First of all, in his opinion, the older communities have their shares assigned to them, and receive their separate princes ; afterwards some of the *prigorodui*, or by-cities, once completely dependent upon the older cities, become stronger than they, and themselves strive after independence. In this way Passek explains the struggle between the old cities of Rostof and Souzdal and the *prigorod* of Vladimir, the " by-city " which developed into the capital. To this opinion Kostomarof would seem to incline.

Bestujef-Riumin, from whom [i. chap. iii. pp. 152—154] this summary is borrowed, says that there can be no doubt that such a fact as the parcelling out of the princely territory ought to be referred to a variety of causes. Each of those already mentioned may have contributed to the general result; but no one of them can be considered as an independent agent, acting with an unmodified force sufficient to bring about the whole result.

The fact that some kind of unity was preserved in Russia during the Appanage period, in spite of the constant feuds and dissensions which then took place, is accounted for—continues Bestujef-Riumin:

I. By the family or clannish relations existing between the different princes.

II. By the prevalence at that time of federal ideas.

III. By the effect produced by compacts entered into by the princes, either among themselves, or with their respective vassals.

The first hypothesis is maintained by Solovief and Kavelin, who suppose that the Varangian Princes, when they came to Russia, accepted the clannish ideas prevalent among the Slavs, and made them the basis of their own mutual relations. In this way was formed the seniority system, according to which a brother inherited before a son (see above, p. 45). After a time the claims of blood-relationship began to be silenced by those of territorial power. In the contest which arose among the members of the princely family, the Princes of Moscow gained the upper hand and became supreme. It is in this way that Solovief accounts for the course taken by early Russian history, and therefore, as he explains everything by internal causes, he attaches but little importance, as regards the development of Russia's political constitution, to the Tartar domination.

The second hypothesis is mainly supported by Kostomarof. It supposes that the Princedoms (or systems of Princedoms) answer to the peoples or tribes (*plemena*) into which the Russian branch of the Slavonic Family was originally divided; and that the Appanage period tied all these separate components into one integral confederation. The idea of a federation was first started by Prince M. M. Shcherbatof, who compared the organization of ancient Russia to that of the Holy Roman Empire; and various writers have attempted, but without much success, to identify the princely with the tribal divisions of Russia. Kostomarof's explanation of what occurred is somewhat different from theirs. Some of the minor nationalities became exhausted or absorbed, while larger ones, formed out of the smaller, grew strong and clearly defined. Of these more powerful nationalities he discerns six: those of (1) South-Russia; (2) the Séverskoe principality ; (3) Great Russia ; (4) White-Russia ; (5) Pskof ; and (6) Novgorod ; and these, he thinks, exist recognizable to the present day.

As regards the third hypothesis, that which ascribes such great influence to treaties or compacts (*dogovornî*), there is no doubt that such compacts did exist in ancient Russia, but it is uncertain when and where they first appeared. The *ryadni* mentioned in the chronicles were not *dogovornî*, though the *ryada* involved the germ of the *dogovor*. The Slavianophiles, indeed, affirm that the basis of the dealings between prince and people was not treaties but mutual trust. With Novgorod and some other great municipalities it is true that princes entered into well-defined agreements ; but the existence of such compacts elsewhere seems almost as doubtful as that of anything like the formal federation claimed for princely Russia by the maintainers of the second hypothesis.

In summing up, Bestujef-Riumin—from whom again [pp. 154—162] I have been borrowing—says that, in his opinion, no one principle can be said to have given rise to the old Russian form of government. On the contrary, the heterogeneous nature of the Russian body politic is to be explained by the variety of principles which were at work while it was being constructed, by the jarring of the complicated interests which at various times affected the progress of the work.

As regards the influence of the appanage system on the fortunes of the land, it seems clear—as has been said above [p. 45]—that it was politically disastrous. It could not but be hurtful also, says Kostomarof [p. 41] to the progress of civilization in Russia. But its influence in this respect, he adds, was not so noxious as was that exercised by the barbarous peoples who successively came into collision with Russia on its eastern and southern frontiers. During the tenth and the first half of the eleventh century the land groaned under the blows inflicted by the Petchenegians. They were succeeded by the Polovtsi ; and before those invaders had long been rendered harmless, the civilization of the country seemed for a time to be on the point of disappearing under the pressure of

III.—THE MONGOL PERIOD.

In speaking of the Asiatic invaders and subjugators of Russia, I have generally called them Tartars,[1] though that designation is of an exceedingly vague character, and has been much abused. The Russian word *Tatarui*, or Tatars,

---

[1] See above, p. 59.

modified in Western Europe by a reference to Tartarus into Tartars, is now generally applied by Russian writers to what used to be the Turkish subjects of the Mongol Empire. It is said to be a corruption of *Tah-tan*, the name under which the Mongols were anciently known to the Chinese.[2] As to the name Mongol, a word of still doubtful extraction, it is said to have been adopted by Genghis Khan. He and his Tartars may possibly not have been Mongols. The Chinese, it seems, consider them to have been Manchoos.

A Chinese contemporary of Genghis Khan (quoted by Vassilief) draws a most unfavourable picture of the Mongols. From his point of view they appeared hideous, filthy, ignorant, lawless barbarians, destitute of respect for age. Nor is the Arabian historian, Ibn-Al-Athír, who died in 1233, much more complimentary, describing them as unclean infidels, who disowned the marriage tie, and were capable even of eating pigs. But of Genghis Khan himself, who is said to have become somewhat civilized during a stay in China as a prisoner,

---

[2] " Tah-tan ; a Mongolic race, dwelling near the Lake Bouyir in Eastern Mongolia." F. Porter Smith's " Vocabulary of Proper Names in Chinese and English," p. 52. Shanghai, 1870. Morrison writes Tătă as Chinese for Tartars.

the Chinese writer speaks in more complimentary terms.

When the Tartars[3] first attacked Russia [see above, pp. 60—62], they seem to have deliberately devastated the land, forming a circle round a district, and then riding into its centre, like beaters at a battue. Towards countries which submitted themselves entirely to their will they did not behave overharshly, always showing a philosophic indifference to what they considered such trifles as the religious or the national prejudices of their subjects; but where they met with opposition, their one remedy was annihilation. Thus during their inroads into Russia they not only swept away every living being they met, but they also destroyed every destructible object which lay in their path. Their policy towards a foe was of a very "thorough" nature.

But except on such occasions, their treatment of the Russian nation in general was not ferocious.

[3] One reason for writing Tartars instead of Mongols is this. The conquerors of Russia doubtless formed part of the Mongol forces, and subjected the country to a distant Mongol Khan; but the tribes which took possession of the country to the South and East of Russia, and became known after a time as the Tartars of the Golden Horde, of Kazan, and of the Crimea, may perhaps have always been of Turkish rather than of Mongolian origin. The Tartars who are now to be seen at Kazan, and in the Crimea, are certainly not Mongols.

On the princes and other leaders of the people, with whom they dealt face to face, their yoke pressed grievously; but the peasantry and the ordinary inhabitants of the towns, during the long intervals between their invasions, can have known them only by hearsay, having about as close an acquaintance with them, in all probability, as English rustics had with the Frenchmen whom they hated during the time of the first Napoleon.

With regard to the influence exercised upon Russia by the Mongols or their Turkish vassals, Russian scholars are at variance. There are some among them who attribute almost as great an importance to the results of the "Mongol yoke" as has been ascribed to it by some foreign writers. There are others who will scarcely acknowledge that it has left behind it even the slightest trace. To the former group belong Karamzin and Kostomarof, who "ascribe to the Tartars a decisive influence upon the development of Russian life." Of the latter group the most important member is Solovief, who "thinks that the influence of the Tartars was not greater than that of the Polovtsi."[4] As usual, Bestujef-Riumin steers a middle course. He admits that the Tartars exercised a consi-

---

[4] Bestujef-Riumin, i. chap. v. p. 272.

derable and permanent influence on the land which, for two centuries and a half, paid them tribute; but he by no means recognizes in a Russian a Tartar cased in an easily scratched-off superficies of civilization. Much that was Oriental seems to have entered, during the time of the long Tartar domination, into the civil administration as well as the military organization of Russia. The minds of men also were greatly affected by the actual horrors perpetrated by the Tartars during their invasions, by the possible risks to which the Russian nation was constantly exposed so long as the Tartar supremacy endured. The princes, being forced to be servile to the Tartars at Sarai or the Mongol Khans in Central Asia, compelled their subjects to be servile to them; and so the spirit of manly independence which appears once to have prevailed throughout Russia, and which continued to manifest itself in Novgorod and Pskof long after it had expired in the rest of the country, became transmuted into a somewhat abject mood of loyalty.

Among the supposed relics of the Tartar period is generally classed the *pravczh*—the means of enforcing payment of debts employed in Russia up to the time of Peter the Great. Of it Fletcher, in his " Russe Common Wealth," gives the following description :—" This *praveush*, or righter, is a place neare to the [law-court or] office ; where such as have sentence passed against them, and refuse to pay that which is adjudged, are beaten with great cudgels on the shinnes and calves of their legges. Every forenoon, from eight to eleven, they are set on the *praveush*, and beate in this sort till the monie be paid. . . . You shall see fortie or fiftie stand together on the *pravcush* all on a rowe, and their shinnes thus becudgelled and bebasted every morning with a piteous crie."[5] But it is impossible, thinks Bestujef-Riumin, to attribute all corporal punishments to the Tartars. " They were well known in Byzantium," he says [i. c. v. p. 279], "and came to us in the codes of ecclesiastical law. They were well known also in the West ; they are found among us in localities, such as Pskof, which were but little subject to the Tartars." The derivation of the word *knut*, or knout, is doubtful, he adds, though it seems closely connected with the German *Knoten*, our knot.

Two of the indirect results of the Tartar domination were of great importance to Russians—the first being the rapid growth of Lithuania ; the second, the steady advancement of Moscow. A

[5] " Russia in the Sixteenth Century," p. 67.

glance at the map will be sufficient to show how monstrous a cantle was cut out of Russia by the Lithuanian princes during the time of the Tartar yoke. The consequences might have been fatal to Russia's independence had not the second result counteracted the first. Russia's loss in extent of territory was compensated by her gain in solidity. The ultimate result of the long-continued Tartar pressure upon the land was the concentration of its strength, the elimination of its weaker elements, the permanent condensation into a stable mass of its previously incoherent particles.

While considering this gloomy period, it may be as well to observe that in the eulogiums generally lavished upon its two chief heroes, Alexander Nefsky and Dimitry Donskoi, Kostomarof seems not altogether inclined to join. He praises, indeed, Alexander's conduct during the earlier part of his life; his brilliant generalship, as displayed against the Swedes, Germans, and Lithuanians. But the Grand Prince's submissive demeanour towards the Tartars appears to be less to the taste of the historian, who evidently suspects a selfish motive for his successful but humiliating policy. But that policy, he says, was entirely in keeping with the teaching of the Church, and therefore it was, he suggests, that the clergy esteemed and lauded him so highly ; and in those days, it must be remembered, the composition of history was a clerical monopoly.

To Dimitry Donskoi Kostomarof evinces even marked hostility, depicting him as a weak, vacillating ruler, always under the influence of some other mind, having neither strength of purpose nor steadiness of aim of his own. His policy he considers disastrous, looking upon Olgerd's invasion of Russia and siege of Moscow as a direct consequence of Dimitry's treatment of Michael of Tver, and on Yagello's alliance with Mamai as being the fruit of Dimitry's behaviour towards Lithuania. Even upon Dimitry's personal courage, as displayed at Kulikovo, Kostomarof throws a doubt [p. 223], and of the Prince's subsequent conduct during Tokhtamish's invasion, he speaks in the severest terms. That invasion, he says, would have produced no evil effect, " had not the Russians been so negligent, and had not the Grand Prince, by his disgraceful flight, abandoned his people to be cut to pieces by barbarians:" the consequence of his want of discernment and resolution being that, after its heroic struggle for independence and its temporary success, the nation had once more to cringe before the Horde.

We have now rapidly passed a second time over several periods of Russian history. We have watched the rise of the principalities of Kief and Vladimir, and we have become acquainted with the state of the country under the Mongol yoke. We will next turn our attention to

IV.—MUSCOVITE RUSSIA.

THE rise of the principality of Moscow has been already described and explained at some length (see above, pp. 124—129). I need not, therefore, dwell long upon it here. But to my account of the opinions upon the subject held by other Russian writers I may add an outline of some of those expressed by Kostomarof in his latest work.

I.

Some Russian historians, he says, have bestowed on Ivan III. the title of "The Great."[1] And undoubtedly we cannot fail to discern that monarch's steadiness of aim and strength of purpose. He understood how to enlarge the boundaries of his realm, to fill his treasure, to concentrate his power. But he did little for the good of the land he ruled. His power became an Asiatic despotism, turning his subjects into timid and silent slaves,

[1] See above, pp. 108—112, 130—134.

while his barbarous punishments developed a taste for coarseness and cruelty among them. His immeasurable greed impoverished the Russian land. Instead of Novgorod becoming richer under the sway of a peace-loving monarch, it was pillaged as though by a band of robbers. At the same time, his behaviour towards the German merchants, and the foreigners who were invited to Moscow, was such as to alienate the class of persons of whom Russia was then specially in need. In all pecuniary transactions he was mean and treacherous, and from him his subjects learnt to be grasping and false and harsh. He made the succession to the throne depend, not on any fixed law, but on the mere will of the reigning monarch; and by this and many similar actions he created in the minds of his people a servile fear of power, but not a manly veneration for established right. A man who is really great is one who advances before others, and leads them after him. But Ivan III. was not in advance of his time. He created a monarchy, but he gave it no impulse towards onward movement in the path of culture: and therefore it remained for two centuries as if petrified, faithful to the pattern given by Ivan, or adding to it merely new forms of a similar type. And so the monarchy could produce nothing until a really great man, Peter I., began to form it into a new state, on an entirely different principle as regarded culture.

In all this there is no doubt a great deal of truth. But Kostomarof seems to be somewhat too severe towards Ivan III., to pay too little consideration, to make too little allowance, for the great difficulties of his position. During a considerable portion of Ivan's reign Russia was struggling for existence. What between the Horde on the one hand and the Polish-Lithuanian power on the other, it was a question whether the isolated Muscovite monarchy could hold its ground. It was not culture that the nation required so much as steady guidance through the storm. Ivan III. was a monarch who in some points resembled Louis XI. We may not be able to discern in him many traces of moral excellence, but that is not a sufficient reason for deeming him devoid of political sagacity.

2.

But with all that Kostomarof says in condemnation of Ivan IV. we may safely coincide. That terrible madman was a disgrace, not only to Russia, but to humanity. There was not really, as some writers have tried to prove, any method in his madness. He seems to have raged, and tortured, and slain, not so much from a desire to serve any private ends, as in obedience to an impulse towards destruction due to a frantic fear. A vision of treachery appears to have been ever before his eyes, a voice counselling destruction never to have ceased ringing in his ears. What is really inexplicable is how it was that he was endured, why his subjects did not rise in just wrath and sweep the monster from off the face of the earth which his presence disgraced. The explanation of this mystery is hard to find. To a certain extent it must be sought in the peculiarities of the Slavonic nature: mild, yielding, easily impressed, and believing implicitly in a destiny against which it is useless to struggle. In part, also, it must be looked for in the devotion to their native and orthodox princes of the members of the Great Russian branch of the Slavonic family, and especially of its Muscovite division. The Grand Prince or Tsar of Moscow was for his subjects something very different from a Constitutional King or an Elective President. He was supposed to reign by the divinest of rights, to be the visible embodiment of the power and will of God. Obedience to him, at all times, under all circumstances, was considered so clearly the first duty of man, that resistance to his will could scarcely occur to a well-regulated Muscovite mind. This servile form of allegiance

P

was partly due to the teaching of the Church. Great as had been the merits of the Clergy in supporting the courage of the nation when all but crushed under the feet of the infidels, so do their demerits appear to have been great, in that they inculcated a perfectly blind obedience, an utterly abject submission, to the orthodox Chief of the State. Here and there a solitary ecclesiastic like the Metropolitan Philip made a noble stand against the ferocious Tsar, and perished a true confessor in the cause of morality and justice. But as a general rule the clergy do not seem to have been able to see with clearer eyes than the great body of the people. Nor was it likely, it must be remembered, that the monarchs would take a less favourable view of their own claims to worship and devotion than was entertained by their subjects. Ivan the Terrible probably believed without a shadow of doubt that he had been invested with despotic power by direct celestial agency, and that all attempts to thwart his purpose or limit his will must be due, at least to infernal suggestion, if not to diabolical support. But even when every modifying influence is taken into consideration, and full attention has been paid to the peculiar features which the case presents, it must remain inconceivable to us, to whom freedom has come as naturally as the light of day or the air we breathe, how men could have witnessed the atrocities committed day after day by the terrible madman upon the throne, and not have made some attempt to stay his destroying hand.

The effect upon the Russian nation of such a system as that which the earlier Grand Princes of Moscow introduced, and the Tsars Ivan III., Vassily Ivanovich, and Ivan the Terrible developed and completed, Kostomarof considers disastrous in the extreme. During a moment of supreme peril, he says, most men become utterly selfish, and under the rule of Ivan III., men's whole lives were spaces of peril. It is not, then, to be wondered at, if. the nation became selfish : when we consider, in addition to this, that under Ivan's successor, Boris Godunof, the mass of the people passed into servitude, we can easily understand how it came about that the moral tone of the Russian people underwent a most unfavourable change.

3.

Very seldom in the history of the world has a monarch ruled so despotically as Ivan IV. Very seldom, also, has a realm been reduced to so disastrous a state of anarchy as that into which Russia drifted after his death. Not only while their sovereign was alive to carry out the promptings of his delirium did the Muscovite Achivi suffer; long after his mania was calmed by death, his evil deeds continued to bear fruit baneful to mankind.

Ivan left behind him two sons. His eldest son, also named Ivan, he had killed during one of his paroxysms of rage. It is said that the Tsar had savagely beaten his daughter-in-law, Prince Ivan's wife. The Prince ventured to remonstrate, and received, by way of reply, a blow which almost instantly deprived him of life. If the stories told about his cruelties are true, his death inflicted no great loss upon the country. Ivan's second son Feodor was feeble-witted, but not otherwise objectionable. The clergy, indeed, won by his sincere piety, deemed him the medium of spiritual communications, and credited him with a gift of second sight due to celestial favour. When the Crimean Tartars attacked Moscow, for instance, the "blessed" Tsar, after having offered up prayers, is said to have predicted the impending discomfiture of the invaders. But the third son of Ivan IV., the young Dimitry, early showed signs of an inclination to follow in the steps of his father of terrible memory. Like Ivan IV., he delighted as a child in tormenting domestic animals. And on one winter's day, it is said, he made a number of snow figures, which he named after Boris Godunof and his chief partisans. Then he beat them, and ordered their hands, their feet, and finally their heads to be struck off, saying the while, " That's what I'll do when I'm in power." It was clear that if he lived he might become dangerous to the royal "innocent" his brother, as well as to the actual ruler of the land, Boris Godunof. To that keen-eyed intriguer, Dimitry's death must have begun to appear not only advantageous but necessary.

How far Boris Godunof was an actually consenting party to the murder of Prince Dimitry, says Kostomarof (p. 584), remains uncertain. Various accounts of that crime have been given, but one of them seems to offer special tokens of authenticity. According to it, the young prince, on the day of his death, felt unwell, but still went to church as usual. On his return home he tasted a *prosfora*, or convent-made loaf, drank some water, and then went out with his nurse. Just as they reached the church of SS. Constantine and Helen they were met by the murderers, who struck her senseless, cut the boy's throat, and then set up an outcry. The Tsaritsa came running out, caught hold of her child by the hand, and found he was dead. " It is evident from this narrative," says Kostomarof, " that there were no actual eye-witnesses of the murder "—except the murderers themselves. The nurse, who was insensible while it was being committed, was taken into custody together with her husband. What became of the unfortunate couple is not known.

4.

Boris Godunof's behaviour on refusing the proffered crown, after the death of Feodor,[2] is singularly like that which the English chroniclers attribute to our Richard III., and with which, following them, Shakespeare has rendered the world familiar.[3] The part played on the English stage by Buckingham is almost identical with that in which the obsequious Patriarch Job figures on the Russian. Just as of Richard it is reported that

> " He is within, with two right reverend fathers,
> Divinely bent to meditation :
> And in no worldly suits would he be moved,
> To draw him from his holy exercise,"—

so we are shown Boris secluded from the world in the Novodévichy Monastery, and protesting against being dragged from his devotions within that tranquil retreat.

Very like Richard's words,

> " For God doth know, and you may partly see,
> How far I am from the desire of this,"

---

[2] See above p. 155.
[3] King Richard III., Act iii. Scene 7.

are those uttered by Boris under similar circumstances :—" Never into my mind has it come, nor will it enter into my thoughts, that I should reign. How could I possibly think of aught so exalted!" And again :—" God is witness .... that such a thought never came into my mind."

As Buckingham entreats Richard to accept the crown, saying,—

" We heartily solicit
Your gracious self to take on you the charge
And kingly government of this your land,"—

so does the Patriarch urge Boris to yield with the words, " Be for us our merciful Gosudar, our Tsar, and Grand Prince:" and as at last Richard exclaims,—

" I am not made of stone,
But penetrable to your kind entreaties,
Albeit against my conscience and my soul,"—

so does Boris, lifting up to heaven eyes streaming with tears, plaintively utter the (already quoted) words, " O Lord God! I am Thy servant. Let Thy will be done!"[4]

There is one striking difference, however, between the two scenes. The English citizens " are mum," and keep silence :

" They spake not a word ;
But like dumb statues or breathing stone,
Stared each on other, and look'd deadly pale."

---

[4] Kostomarof, i. 593. Solovief, viii. 10.

Nor does Buckingham venture to use violence towards them. But the Moscovite townspeople are forced by threats and blows to prostrate themselves before their future lord, and to weep and howl aloud. And when at length Boris consents to accept the weighty honour thrust upon him, they all cry, " Glory to God ! "—his agents thumping them the while, " in order," says the annalist, " that they may shout louder and more joyfully."

5.

Who the first "False Demetrius" really was[5] Kostomarof finds himself unable to decide. It is not probable, he says, that if the real Prince Dimitry had been saved from the hands of the assassins, his preservers would have allowed him to lead an obscure and degrading life in Russian monasteries or in Polish mansions. They would surely have handed him over to King Sigismund of Poland, who would have been delighted to obtain so valuable a hostage as the childless Tsar's only brother. Even suppose they had their reasons for keeping his existence a secret in Feodor's lifetime, what could have prevented them from disclosing it after that Tsar's death, and during the period of Boris Godunof's feigned reluctance to mount the throne ?

[5] See above, p. 160.

Some writers have been so much impressed by the frank and apparently honest demeanour of the Pretender, that they have come to the conclusion that, at all events, he must have been brought up in, and must have held, the belief that he was the son of Ivan III. This opinion Kostomarof thinks would be entitled to carry weight, if it were not for the following reason :—From Sigismund's letters it is clear that the Claimant professed to have been saved from death exactly at the time when the supposed murder took place at Uglitch. But at that time Prince Dimitry was eight years old. It seems scarcely credible that any one could have been made to believe that up to his eighth year he was surrounded by persons of whom, and by objects of which, he had not the slightest recollection. It may be replied, however, that his instructors may have persuaded him that he was less than eight years old when the events in question took place, and he may have accepted their whole story in good faith. If that was the case, says Kostomarof, the chances are that his educators in the belief that he was the Prince were those Polish nobles who originally took up his cause, and who after his death recognized and supported other assumers of Dimitry's name. After all, Kostomarof points out, the Pretender was not perfectly free from hypocrisy; as is proved by the fact of his showing favour to Molchanof, one of the murderers of Boris Godunof's widow and son, while he professed to lament their untimely fate.

Boris and the Patriarch Job gave out that the Pretender was the runaway monk, Grigory Otrepief. At a later period Shouisky made the same statement, and supported it by the evidence of Varlaam, one of that monk's fellow-travellers. Against this Otrepief-hypothesis may be urged the following arguments:—

1. If the Pretender was the Otrepief who absconded from Moscow in 1602, he could have had only two years at the outside in which to complete his education. It seems incredible that in that short space of time a runaway Russian monk could have been turned into so complete a Polish noble as the Pretender was, who is known to have been a model rider, dancer, swordsman, and shot, and to have spoken Polish to perfection, whereas his Russian was not quite free from suspicion. On the day of his arrival in Moscow, moreover, when he saluted the holy pictures, it was remarked that he did not seem to know exactly how to behave. A Russian who had been brought up in a monastery could scarcely have been at a loss how to greet a Church picture.

2. The Pretender brought with him a man whom he exhibited in public as Grigory Otrepief. It was said afterwards that this man was not the real Otrepief, but an impostor—whom some identified as a monk called Leonidas, others as a monk called Pimen. But the real Grigory Otrepief was a well-known personage. As secretary to the Patriarch Job he often attended the meetings of the Council, and many of the nobles were personally acquainted with him. He used to live, moreover, in the monastery of which Paphnutius was Archimandrite. If the Pretender had been Otrepief, he would have been likely to keep Paphnutius at a distance, whereas that ecclesiastic continued to act throughout the whole of the Pretender's eleven months' reign as a member of the Senate, and was thus daily brought into personal contact with him.

3. In one of the Volhynian monasteries there is a book which contains the autograph of Grigory Otrepief. In that autograph there cannot be detected the least similarity to the Pretender's handwriting.[6]

Some Russian writers have attributed the fall of the "False Demetrius" entirely to his own behaviour. According to them, the people rebelled

[6] Kostomarof, i. 629—631.

against him, and put him to death, having been
alienated from him by his neglect of his religious
duties, and his manifest leaning towards Rome and
Poland. But this Kostomarof denies. According
to him, the Pretender had not in any way shocked
the mass of the people, although he had greatly
displeased the representatives of the extreme Con-
servative party. His fall was not due to any up-
rising of an angry people. It was entirely the
result of a conspiracy set on foot by a few nobles,
and headed by that one among them who afterwards
succeeded to the throne. The great body of the
people remained faithful to their allegiance, as is
proved by the fact that they afterwards enthusias-
tically supported the impostor who pretended to
be their Tsar Dimitry—who, it was said, had
escaped from death on the morning of the 17th of
May, 1606, as he had previously escaped at Uglitch
in 1591.[7]

6.

Vassily Shouisky, who succeeded to the throne
on the death of the "False Demetrius," was in
politics the exact opposite of that enigmatical personage. He was the type, according to Kosto-

[7] Kostomarof, i. 664.

marof, of that phase of Russian Conservatism which was due to the influence of Asiatic stagnation. " We see in him," says that historian [i. 665], " an absence of all spirit of enterprise, a dread of every novel step, but at the same time endurance and perseverance—Russian qualities which constantly astonished foreigners. He bowed his neck before superior force, obediently served power while it was strong, and studiously avoided any chance of coming into collision with it; but as soon as he saw it growing weak he turned against it, and joined others in hewing down that which he had been wont to worship."

When the people began to rise against the Godunof family, Shouisky tried to quiet them, affirming that the Pretender was the runaway monk Otrepief; when the Pretender's star appeared to be in the ascendant, Shouisky went over to his side, and so precipitated the fall of the reigning dynasty; when an opportunity presented itself of depriving the Pretender at the same time of his sceptre and his life, Shouisky seized it, and turned it to his own advantage.

He mounted the vacant throne, but his election was not of a quite satisfactory nature. After some debate the boyars agreed to elect him Tsar, on condition that he would rule in accordance with their wishes. The people were summoned by the sound of the tocsin into the great square. Shouisky's partizans immediately hailed him as Tsar. Some persons affirmed that all the Muscovite towns ought to be summoned to send up deputies to elect a successor to the throne. But the boyars declared that this was unnecessary, and Shouisky was at once sworn in. After he had taken the prescribed oath, by which he bound himself to observe various conditions, the boyars swore allegiance to him. Afterwards a message was sent to all the towns, by which it was affirmed that Vassily Ivanovich Shouisky had been elected to the throne by common consent, on the ground of his descent from the Souzdal Princes and his relationship to St. Alexander Nefsky. It proceeded to say that the late occupant of the throne had been an impostor, heretical, given to diabolical practices, desirous of upsetting the orthodox faith and introducing Romanism and Lutheranism, and evilly-minded towards the boyars and other councillors of state.

But in spite of all these assertions, the people, as we have already seen,[8] did not take kindly to Shouisky. On the occasion of the translation of Prince Dimitry's remains from Uglitch the mob showed signs of an inclination to stone their new Tsar. A

[8] See above, p. 166—168.

little later, when the air was full of rumours of a coming Dimitry, all Russia was ready to desert the reigning monarch. After a brief period of encouragement the Tsar was obliged to give up all hopes of maintaining himself upon the throne. And so "he laid aside his sceptre, and retired from the royal palace into his own house."

The election of Prince Ladislas, son of the Polish King Sigismund, was as irregular as had been that of Shouisky. In presence of Zolkiewski and his Polish troops, the principal boyars could not refuse to acknowledge the claims of Ladislas, and accordingly that foreign prince was proclaimed Tsar on certain conditions. But the consent of the nation was neither asked nor given, though at a later period the Russian towns, one after another, swore allegiance to Ladislas. Had Sigismund at once supported his son, instead of striving to get his kingdom for himself, the hold of Ladislas upon the Russian sceptre might have become assured.

We have already seen [p. 174] how the country at length put forth its strength and freed itself from its foreign yoke. It is unfortunate that the details of the election to the vacant throne which followed are not fully known. It was soon after the 21st of December that the towns were summoned to send up deputies to Moscow for the purpose of electing a tsar. The deputies arrived, and several fruitless sittings took place. Then a three days' fast was observed throughout the country, and prayers were solemnly offered up in the churches, beseeching God to enlighten the minds of the deputies; so that their task of electing a tsar might be accomplished, not according to human guile, but in accordance with the Divine Will. When the Assembly met again after these pious proceedings had taken place, a proposal was made to elect a Swedish prince. But the deputies with one voice exclaimed that they were not going to choose a foreigner to rule over them. Then various boyars were mentioned, some of whom, it is said, had obtained certain votes by means of bribes. At length the name of Michael Romanof began to be mentioned with favour on all sides.

The founder of the Romanof family, says Kostomarof,[1] was a certain emigrant from the Prussian land, named Andrei Ivanovich Kobyla. His fifth son, a renowned boyar, named Fedor Koshka left four sons. The eldest of these also, Ivan by name, had four sons. The youngest of these, Zachary, left a family which received from him the surname of Zacharin.

[1] Kostomarof, i. 729—733.

Zachary's second son, Yury or George, left children, one of whom was called Roman. Roman had a daughter, Anastasia,—who became the first wife of Ivan the Terrible—and a son, Nikita. From the time of this Nikita Romanovich, the family was known as that of Romanof. Nikita had several sons. The fact of their aunt having been the wife of Ivan IV. caused them to be suspected by Boris Godunof, who banished one of them, Alexander, to the shores of the White Sea, and imprisoned two others, Vassily and Michael. Alexander is said to have been strangled. Vassily soon died in consequence of the severe treatment to which he was subjected. Michael was immured in a dungeon, in which he died; to this day the heavy chains he wore are preserved in a neighbouring church. Another brother, Ivan, was banished, but outlived his exile. One brother remained—Fedor Nikitich Romanof. No handsomer cavalier, no better horseman was to be found in all Moscow than he. He was married to a lady named Ksenia Ivanovna Shestova, and had two young children; a boy named Michael, and a girl. Suddenly, by Boris Godunof's commands, this gay cavalier, this happy husband and father, was torn from his wife and children, and forced to become a monk. The name of Filaret was assigned to him, and he was placed under the inspection of a keeper, who was ordered to report every deed, every word of his, to Boris. His wife was forced to become a nun, bearing in religion the name of Marfa, and was banished to a convent in the neighbourhood of Lake Onega, while his children were sent away with an aunt to Béloozero. Bitterly, according to his keeper's reports, did the solitary monk Filaret grieve over the dear ones he had lost. " Woe is me for my wife and children!" would he cry. "When I think of them, it is as though a spear went through my heart. Would that God had rather taken them to himself!" For some time he was kept in ignorance of their fate, but at length a priest and some peasants, belonging to the district to which his wife had been sent, contrived to let him know where she was, and to convey to her tidings about him.

In 1605, during the height of the contest between Boris Godunof and the " False Demetrius," Filaret suddenly changed the submissive tone he had adopted for one of defiance, threatening the monastic authorities—his keeper reports—and showing an inclination to beat them, saying the while, " You will see what I shall become by and by." Then came the overthrow of Boris Godunof, bringing with it the recall to the busy world of the two surviving Romanofs. Ivan was made a boyar, and Filaret became Metropolitan of Rostof.

While the Russian towns were one after another submitting to the Pretender generally known as the Tushino Rogue, Filaret kept Rostof faithful to Shouisky. On the 11th of October, 1608, a number of the Pretender's partisans, some of them detached from the Polish army just then besieging the Troitsa Monastery, suddenly fell upon Rostof, dragged the Metropolitan from the cathedral, and carried him off to the Pretender's camp at Tushino. There he remained for some time, but at length he was able to escape. After Shouisky's forced abdication, Filaret and some others were commissioned to treat with the Polish king Sigismund. At first the envoys were well received, but after a time they were sent as prisoners to Warsaw, and there long detained in captivity.

It was during this period that the deputies assembled at Moscow in order to elect a monarch, and the name of Filaret's son Michael began to be uttered as that of the future Tsar. At length, after many delays, the final sitting took place on the first Sunday in Lent, February 21, 1613. Each order gave its vote in writing, and all the votes were found to be in favour of electing Michael Fedorovich Romanof. Then the Archbishop of

Riazan, the Cellarer of the Troitsa, the Archimandrite of the Novospassky Monastery, and the boyar Morozof, went out to the great square in front of the Kremlin, and asked the assembled multitudes whom they wished to have for their Tsar. And "Michael Fedorovich Romanof" was their reply.

V. SERFDOM.

There is one most important chapter of Russian history which I have left all but untouched; that which tells how the peasantry of Russia, of old absolutely free, then subject to certain slight restraints upon their liberty of action, at length became slaves.

This sad chapter does not belong to the early history of the nation; it dates only from the time when Boris Godunof, murderer and usurper, began to exercise his sinister and disastrous influence upon the fortunes of the land. By him serfdom is generally supposed to have been introduced into Russia; after him it lasted for rather more than two centuries and a half.

Into the question of its merits and demerits I will not now enter. Nor will I here discuss the political or economical effects of its recent abolition;[1]

[1] These will, I believe, be fully discussed in a forthcoming

but on its social and moral results I cannot but say a few parting words.

While allowing that the Russian peasant has certain good qualities—such as kindness, patience, endurance, domestic affection, respect for age, obedient submission to the Church, loyal devotion towards the throne—many writers have yet spoken of him harshly, charging him with idleness, drunkenness, falsehood, dishonesty, and a total disregard of economical precepts. Of these charges it is impossible utterly to acquit the Russian peasantry. But many extenuating circumstances may be pleaded in their favour. It is hard for a man who lives in perpetual insecurity and dread, to work with the steady perseverance which a life of fearless security promotes. It is hard for a slave, liable to be treated every moment with contumely and blows, to maintain that feeling of self-respect which renders a man superior to many of the temptations which beset poverty: to the dreariness which finds a solace in drink, to the weakness which suggests words of falsehood and acts of dishonesty, to the acute despair which goads its victim into deadly

---

work by Mr. Mackenzie Wallace. He has devoted four years to the task of studying Russian institutions on their native soil, working with a conscientious industry which is certain to bear good fruit.

crime. Hard is it, moreover, for one whose little all is at the mercy of a harsh taskmaster, to accustom himself to those habits of self-denying frugality in which the independent peasantry of many lands are trained. Under the new order of things, let us hope, the working classes of Russia will rise as high in moral tone as in social position, above their long-afflicted forefathers.

As to their own opinion about the change which has taken place in their treatment, as well as to the view which we ought to take of it, all I have to say is this. Let us suppose for a moment that a total eclipse of the sun takes place, and endures for long years : that men become accustomed to live in an almost complete absence of light, to grow up ignorant of colour, and only dimly conscious of form. And suppose that after a long period of this continual darkness the eclipsing cause is suddenly removed, and the gladdened world is bathed in a welcome flood of sunlight, and the eyes of men can indulge in a long-denied feast of colour, and to their ears is borne the long-silenced voice of woodland song. Then it is possible that, amid the busy hum of general gratitude and congratulation, may be heard some notes of discontent. Eyes that have become purblind during the long eclipse may smart beneath the searching rays of the sun, ears that the nocturnal silence has soothed may be deafened by the unwonted clamour of the day. Here may some poverty-stricken wretch be heard complaining of the far too candid light which has revealed the nakedness over which has hitherto been drawn the discreet mantle of darkness: there may a husband be seen lost in dismay at the ungainliness of a wife who in the twilight had appeared attractive. But we may be sure that under such circumstances the vast majority of mankind, and we ourselves among them, would most decidedly hail the kindly light, and look back with a shudder upon the period of eclipse to which its returning rays had put an end.

In like manner it is possible that among the older members of the Russian peasantry there may exist some fond recollection of the good old times when they were treated like domestic animals— that is to say, with an amount of attention often not lavished by men upon their fellow-creatures. But we may be sure that before many years have passed away there will have died out of the Russian mind all yearning after the material advantages of servitude. In the meantime there can be no doubt as to the side which, in this conflict of freedom with slavery, should enlist our own sympathies. As to the eyes of all but overweary men the daylight must ever seem more welcome than the darkness, so to English hearts, must the restored freedom of the Russian land appear beyond all comparison preferable to the servitude under which it was doomed to groan, from the dark days of Boris Godunof to the sunnier times of Alexander the Second.

www.ingramcontent.com/pod-product-compliance
Lightning Source LLC
Chambersburg PA
CBHW022007220426
43663CB00007B/999